# Microsoft® Office Word 2013: Part 1

# Microsoft® Office Word 2013: Part 1

Part Number: 091024
Course Edition: 2.1

## Acknowledgements

### PROJECT TEAM

| Author | Media Designer | Content Editor |
|---|---|---|
| Micky Markert | Alex Tong | Joe McElveney |
| Gail Sandler | | Tricia Murphy |

## Notices

### DISCLAIMER

### TRADEMARK NOTICES

# Microsoft® Office Word 2013: Part 1

# About This Course

These days, most people take electronic word-processing for granted. While we may still write out our grocery lists with pen and paper, we expect to use a computer to create the majority of our documents. It's impossible to avoid word-processing software in many areas of the business world. Managers, lawyers, clerks, reporters, and editors rely on this software to do their jobs. Whether you are an executive secretary or a website designer, you'll need to know the ins and outs of electronic word-processing.

Microsoft® Word 2013 is designed to help you move smoothly through the task of creating professional-looking documents. Its rich features and powerful tools can make your work easy, and even fun. In this course, you'll learn how to use Word 2013 to create and edit simple documents; format documents; add tables and lists; add design elements and layout options; and proof documents.

You can also use this course to prepare for the Microsoft Office Specialist (MOS) Certification exams for Microsoft Word 2013.

## Course Description

### Target Student

This course is intended for students who want to learn basic Word 2013 skills, such as creating, editing, and formatting documents; inserting simple tables and creating lists; and employing a variety of techniques for improving the appearance and accuracy of document content.

### Course Prerequisites

To ensure success, students should be familiar with using personal computers, and should have experience using a keyboard and mouse. Students should be comfortable in the Windows® 8 environment, and be able to use Windows 8 to manage information on their computers. Specific tasks the students should be able to perform include: launching and closing applications, navigating basic file structures, and managing files and folders. To meet this prerequisite, you can take any one or more of the following Logical Operations courses:

- *Using Microsoft® Windows® 8*
- *Microsoft® Windows® 8: Transition from Windows® 7*

### Course Objectives

In this course, you will learn fundamental Word 2013 skills. You will start by getting acquainted with the Word user interface, creating a new document, and finding help. You will find, select, and modify text. You'll format text as well as paragraphs, and add tables to documents. You'll manage more complicated lists, and insert graphic objects. You'll apply design and layout options to pages. You'll check your documents for spelling, grammar, and other errors, and use other proofing tools to look up information. Finally, you'll customize the Word environment to better suit your individual work habits, and learn additional methods of saving documents.

You will:

- Identify the various components of the Word interface, create a new Word document, enter text into a document, save a document, preview and print a document, and search Help.
- Navigate through a document to find and select text, modify selected text, and find and replace text.
- Apply character formatting to text, align paragraphs using tab stops, display text as list items, control paragraph layout, apply borders and shading to paragraphs, apply text styles, and manage formatting in documents.
- Insert a table into a document, modify the structure of a table, format a table, and convert text to a table.
- Sort a list, renumber a list, and customize a list.
- Insert symbols and special characters, and add images to a document.
- Apply page borders and colors, apply a watermark, add a header and footer to a document, and control page layout.
- Check spelling and grammar and use other proofing tools.
- Customize the Word interface and use additional options for saving.

## The LogicalCHOICE Home Screen

The LogicalCHOICE Home screen is your entry point to the LogicalCHOICE learning experience, of which this course manual is only one part. Visit the LogicalCHOICE Course screen both during and after class to make use of the world of support and instructional resources that make up the LogicalCHOICE experience.

http://www.lo-choice.com

Log-on and access information for your LogicalCHOICE environment will be provided with your class experience. On the LogicalCHOICE Home screen, you can access the LogicalCHOICE Course screens for your specific courses.

Each LogicalCHOICE Course screen will give you access to the following resources:

- eBook: an interactive electronic version of the printed book for your course.
- LearnTOs: brief animated components that enhance and extend the classroom learning experience.

Depending on the nature of your course and the choices of your learning provider, the LogicalCHOICE Course screen may also include access to elements such as:

- The interactive eBook.
- Social media resources that enable you to collaborate with others in the learning community using professional communications sites such as LinkedIn or microblogging tools such as Twitter.
- Checklists with useful post-class reference information.
- Any course files you will download.
- The course assessment.
- Notices from the LogicalCHOICE administrator.
- Virtual labs, for remote access to the technical environment for your course.
- Your personal whiteboard for sketches and notes.
- Newsletters and other communications from your learning provider.
- Mentoring services.
- A link to the website of your training provider.
- The LogicalCHOICE store.

Visit your LogicalCHOICE Home screen often to connect, communicate, and extend your learning experience!

# How to Use This Book

## As You Learn

This book is divided into lessons and topics, covering a subject or a set of related subjects. In most cases, lessons are arranged in order of increasing proficiency.

The results-oriented topics include relevant and supporting information you need to master the content. Each topic has various types of activities designed to enable you to practice the guidelines and procedures as well as to solidify your understanding of the informational material presented in the course. Procedures and guidelines are presented in a concise fashion along with activities and discussions. Information is provided for reference and reflection in such a way as to facilitate understanding and practice.

Data files for various activities as well as other supporting files for the course are available by download from the LogicalCHOICE Course screen. In addition to sample data for the course exercises, the course files may contain media components to enhance your learning and additional reference materials for use both during and after the course.

At the back of the book, you will find a glossary of the definitions of the terms and concepts used throughout the course. You will also find an index to assist in locating information within the instructional components of the book.

## As You Review

Any method of instruction is only as effective as the time and effort you, the student, are willing to invest in it. In addition, some of the information that you learn in class may not be important to you immediately, but it may become important later. For this reason, we encourage you to spend some time reviewing the content of the course after your time in the classroom.

## As a Reference

The organization and layout of this book make it an easy-to-use resource for future reference. Taking advantage of the glossary, index, and table of contents, you can use this book as a first source of definitions, background information, and summaries.

## Course Icons

Watch throughout the material for these visual cues:

| Icon | Description |
|------|-------------|
| | A **Note** provides additional information, guidance, or hints about a topic or task. |
| | A **Caution** helps make you aware of places where you need to be particularly careful with your actions, settings, or decisions so that you can be sure to get the desired results of an activity or task. |
| | **LearnTO** notes show you where an associated LearnTO is particularly relevant to the content. Access LearnTOs from your LogicalCHOICE Course screen. |
| | **Checklists** provide job aids you can use after class as a reference to performing skills back on the job. Access checklists from your LogicalCHOICE Course screen. |
| | **Social** notes remind you to check your LogicalCHOICE Course screen for opportunities to interact with the LogicalCHOICE community using social media. |
| | **Notes Pages** are intentionally left blank for you to write on. |

# 1 Getting Started with Word

**Lesson Time: 1 hour, 15 minutes**

## Lesson Objectives

In this lesson, you will:

- Identify the basic elements of the Word application window.

- Create a new document, enter text into a document, save a document, and preview and print a document.

- Search the Help feature for information about a specific Word topic.

## Lesson Introduction

Microsoft® Word 2013 is a word-processing application that helps you create and edit documents of all kinds, from standard business forms to newsletters and blog posts. A necessary step whenever learning a new application is to familiarize yourself with the user interface. Knowing how to move around in a program before you start working in it can save you time you might otherwise waste in hunting for the right button to click or the right place to search for help. This lesson will help you identify and use some of the basic tools and features of the Word 2013 interface.

# TOPIC A

## Identify the Components of the Word Interface

You've probably opened a new software program for the first time and been puzzled by all the unfamiliar elements on the screen. How do I begin working in this program? What happens if I click that button? What does this icon represent? When you begin the process of learning a new program, it's helpful to first acquaint yourself with the components and tools that make the program work. Then, you can jump into your tasks, knowing where to go and how to get there.

### Word 2013

Word 2013 is part of Microsoft Office 2013, a suite of applications for creating documents, spreadsheets, presentations, and databases. You can use Word to quickly and easily create and edit many different types of documents, such as reports, newsletters, and web pages. Word provides tools that help you make the most of your ideas, and will ensure that the content of your documents is not only accurate, but readable and professional.

Word 2013 opens to a *landing page*. This page enables you to open existing documents or create new documents. The first time you open Word 2013, you might be prompted to configure the theme or look for the application. You might also be prompted to identify yourself through a Microsoft account or other authentication method. You can use the **Switch account** link to change which user is logged in from the landing page as well.

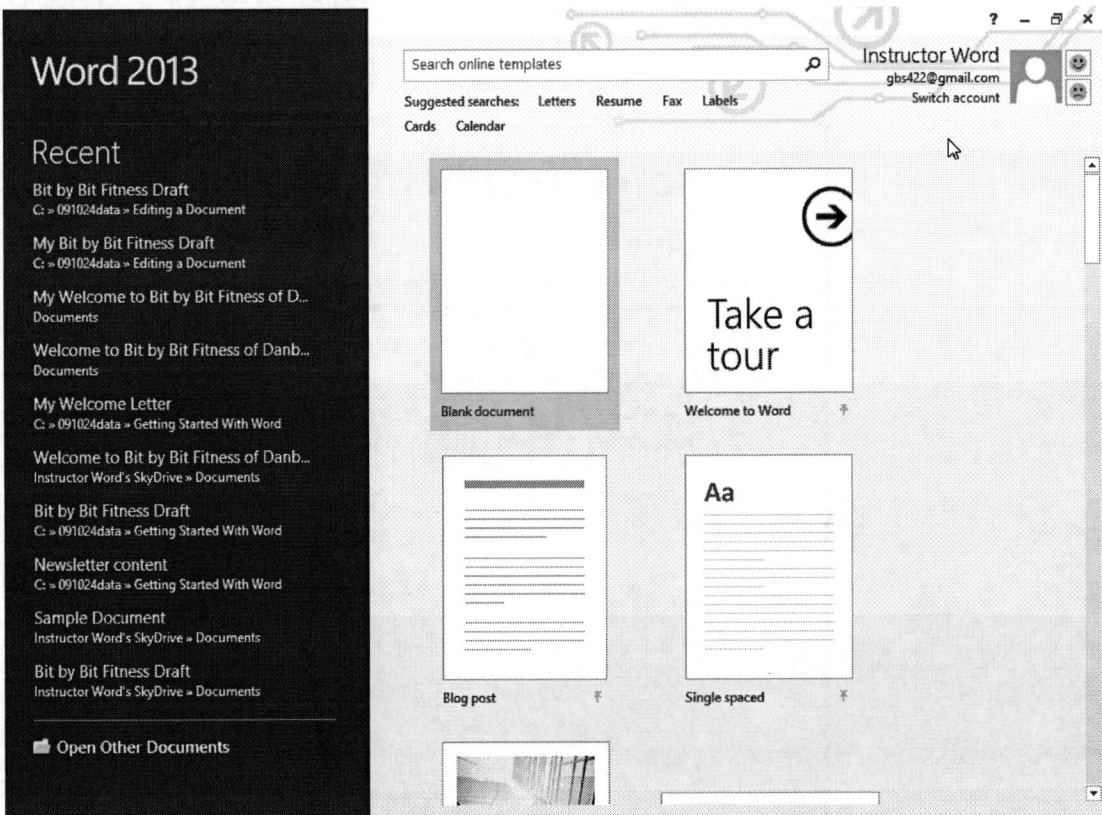

*Figure 1–1: The Word 2013 landing page.*

## Word Documents

A *Word document* is an electronic document created by the Word application. It can contain one page or many pages. It can contain text, graphics, tables, and charts. It can be edited and enhanced to your specifications. Word documents can be stored on your computer, emailed, or printed.

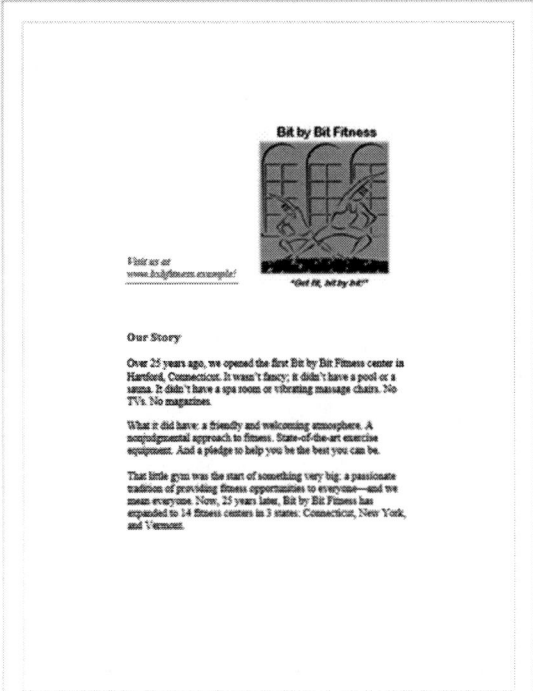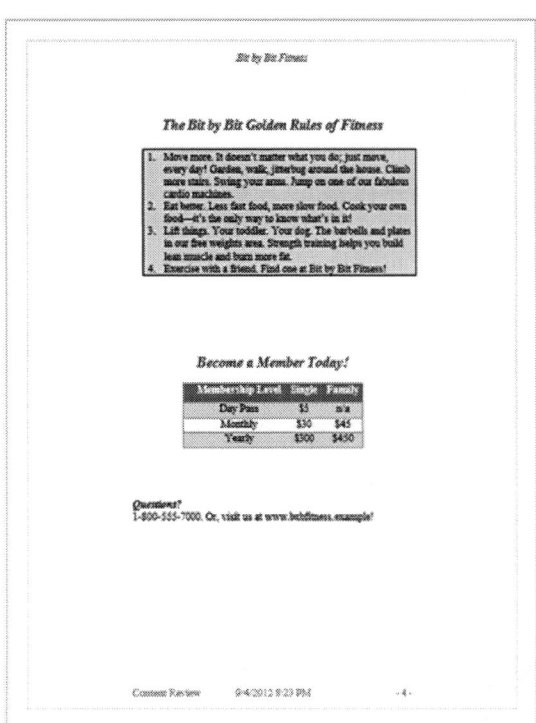

*Figure 1-2: Word document showing text, picture, and table.*

## The Word Application Window

The Word application window contains tools you'll use to work with documents. In the application window, you display and edit a document, and use various features to enhance the appearance of your document.

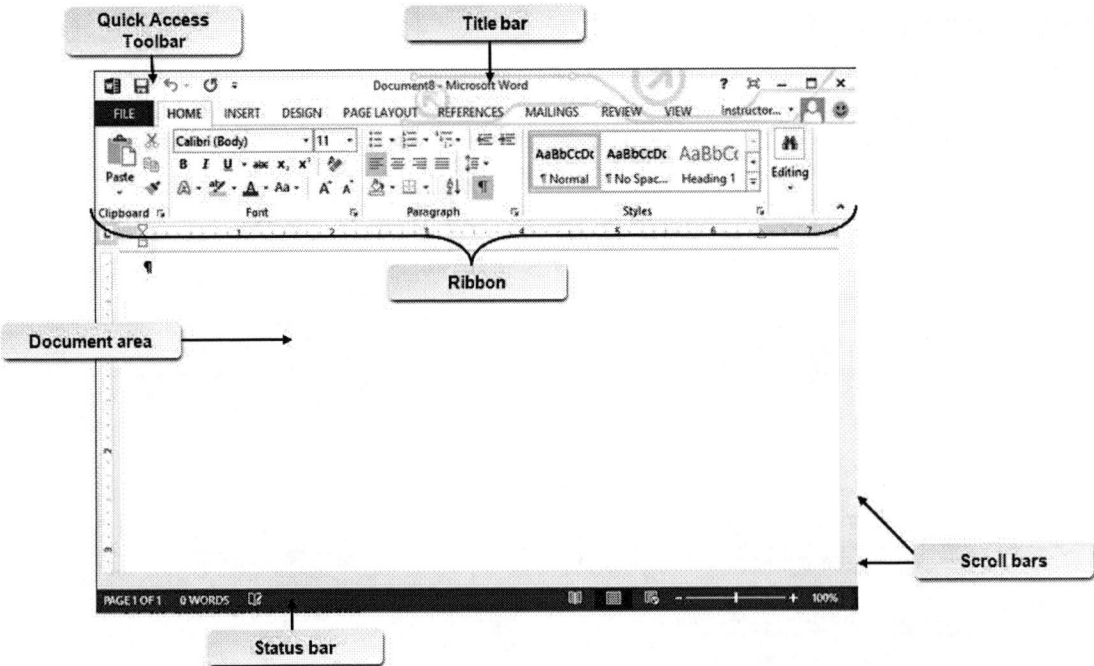

*Figure 1–3: Word 2013 interface components.*

The following table describes some of the core components of the Word application window.

| Component | Description |
|---|---|
| **Quick Access Toolbar** | Located in the uppermost left of the window. The **Quick Access Toolbar** provides one-click access to core commands such as **Save**, **Undo**, and **Redo**. It can also be customized to include additional commands based on user preference. |
| Title bar | Located along the top of the window. The title bar displays the name of the current document. |
| Ribbon | Located directly below the title bar. The ribbon contains common commands and features used to create and edit documents. |
| Document area | The main portion of the window. The document area is where you display documents. |
| Scroll bars | Located to the right of and directly under the document area. The scroll bars allow you to navigate a document vertically or horizontally. |
| Status bar | Located along the bottom of the window. The status bar shows information about the current document, such as the number of pages or words. |

## The Ribbon

The ribbon is a graphical menu panel that appears at the top of the application window. It was designed to provide a central location for accessing various functions of the environment without having to navigate the user interface extensively. From the ribbon, you can access most, if not all, of the commands that you will need to use in the application.

The ribbon is made up of two parts: the tabs and the command groups that make up each tab. Each tab has an organizational title that references the specific functions that the command groups within that tab provide. Each command group also has an organizational title, with the specific commands within each group associated with a specific task in the application environment. You can customize the ribbon by adding, removing, or rearranging tabs, groups, and commands.

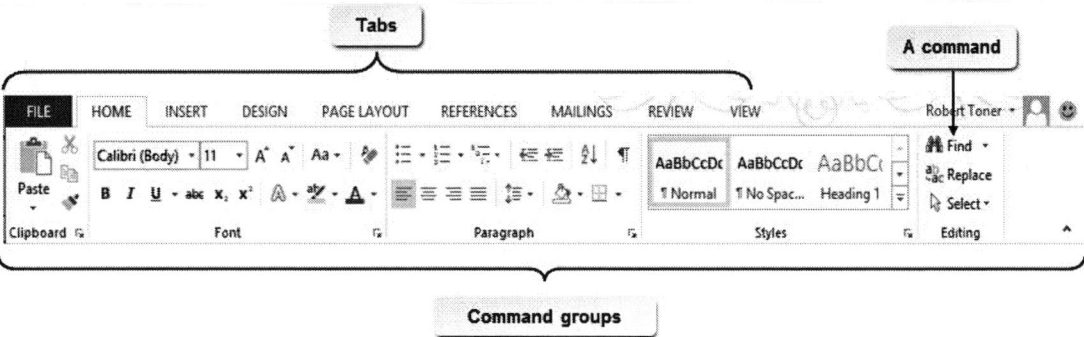

*Figure 1-4: The components of the ribbon in Word 2013.*

Each ribbon tab provides access to commands used to perform specific actions in the Word 2013 application.

| Tab | Description |
| --- | --- |
| FILE | Displays the **Backstage View**, where you can access commands that perform file-related tasks, such as saving and printing. On the **FILE** tab, you can also get information about a document, and configure Word customization options. |
| HOME | Contains the frequently used commands you'll use to start working with a Word document. The command groups on this tab include **Clipboard**, **Font**, **Paragraph**, **Styles**, and **Editing**. They allow you to format and edit text. |
| INSERT | Contains commands that insert different objects into your document, such as charts, tables, and pictures. Groups on this tab include **Pages**, **Tables**, **Illustrations**, **Links**, **Header & Footer**, **Text**, and **Symbols**. |
| DESIGN | Contains commands that enable you to make design changes to your document including setting document themes, colors and fonts, paragraph spacing, watermarks, page color, and page borders. The groups on this tab include **Document Formatting** and **Page Background**. |
| PAGE LAYOUT | Contains commands used to customize document pages, including controlling the placement of text and graphics. Groups on this tab include **Themes**, **Page Setup**, **Page Background**, **Paragraph**, and **Arrange**. |
| REFERENCES | Contains commands to create references to the document content, such as footnotes and indexes. Groups on this tab include **Table of Contents**, **Footnotes**, **Citations & Bibliography**, **Captions**, **Index**, and **Table of Authorities**. |
| MAILINGS | Contains commands to create mailing documents, such as faxes, letters, and emails. Groups on this tab include **Create**, **Start Mail Merge**, **Write & Insert Fields**, **Preview Results**, and **Finish**. |
| REVIEW | Contains commands to review and edit the content in a document. Groups on this tab include **Proofing**, **Comments**, **Language**, **Tracking**, **Changes**, **Compare**, and **Protect**. |

| Tab | Description |
| --- | --- |
| VIEW | Contains various commands to switch between different document views. Groups on this tab include **Document Views**, **Show**, **Zoom**, **Window**, and **Macros**. |

### Hide or Pin the Ribbon

By default, the ribbon is displayed. If you want more room on your screen to view the document, you can hide the ribbon until you need it. Select the ^ at the far right of the ribbon to hide it. To display it again, select one of the tab titles. After you select the desired command from the ribbon, it will be hidden again. If you want to keep the ribbon open after hiding it, select a tab title, then click the **Pin the ribbon** button at the far right of the ribbon.

### ScreenTips

A *ScreenTip* appears when you hover the mouse pointer over commands on the ribbon and certain other elements of the application window. The command ScreenTip provides a brief description of the command, and, where applicable, the keyboard shortcut used to execute the command.

### Dialog Box Launchers

*Dialog box launchers* are small buttons with downward-pointing arrows located in the bottom-right corner of some groups on the ribbon. When selected, they open dialog boxes or task panes containing commands specific to the features of that group. Some dialog boxes and task panes contain advanced commands not available on the ribbon.

 **Note:** To further explore the ribbon, you can access the LearnTO **Navigate the Office 2013 Ribbon** presentation from the **LearnTO** tile on the LogicalCHOICE Course screen.

## The Backstage View

The *Backstage View* in Word is the "behind the scenes" view of commands you can use to do file-related tasks, such as saving, opening, or printing a document. You access the **Backstage View** by selecting the **FILE** tab on the ribbon.

The **Backstage View** will also show information about the current document, such as the date it was created, or its permissions status. Other tabs in the **Backstage View** allow you to send a document via email, convert a document to a different file format, and customize the way Word behaves.

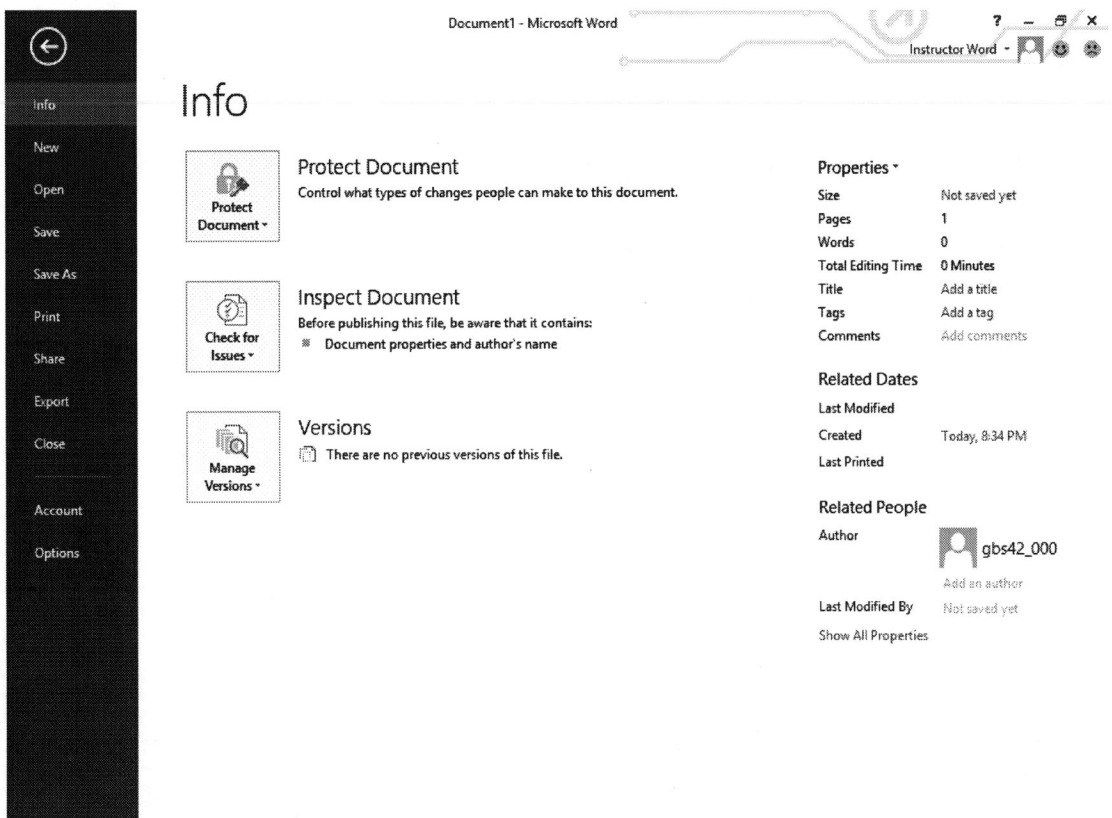

*Figure 1-5: The Backstage View.*

## Task Panes

A *task pane* provides quick access to feature-specific options and commands. A task pane can be resized, moved, and kept open while working on a document. Task panes can be opened either by using commands on the ribbon, such as dialog box launchers, or from within other task panes.

## Galleries

A *gallery* is a collection of elements that belong to the same category, such as styles or effects. Galleries display preset styles you can select from, offering a quick way to change the appearance of your document. You access galleries by selecting the down arrow that appears to the right of the ribbon element associated with the gallery.

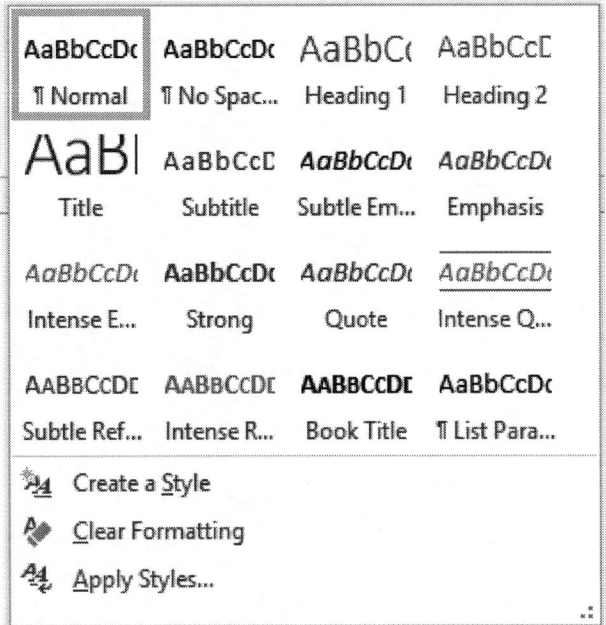

*Figure 1–6: The Quick Styles gallery.*

 **Access the Checklist tile on your LogicalCHOICE course screen for reference information and job aids on How to Work with Components of the Word Application Window**

# ACTIVITY 1-1

## Working with Components of the Word Application Window

### Scenario

Bit by Bit Fitness is a growing company with fitness centers in three states: Vermont, New York, and Connecticut. You've just taken a job as an assistant to the manager of the Danbury center. Your boss has recently installed Microsoft Office 2013, and you want to get up to speed with it immediately, so you decide to take the time to become familiar with the application window.

1. Explore the ribbon.

    **Note:** This course uses a streamlined notation for ribbon commands. They'll appear as "[Ribbon Tab]→[Group]→[Button or Control]" as in "select HOME→Clipboard→Paste." If the group name isn't needed for navigation or there isn't a group, it's omitted, as in "select FILE→Open."

   a) On the **Start** page, select **Word 2013**.

       **Note:** If **Word 2013** is not listed on the **Start** page, right-click a blank area, then at the bottom of the window select **All apps**.

   b) If necessary, in the **User Name** dialog box, select **OK** or enter the appropriate Microsoft account, and then select **OK**.
      Word 2013 opens to the landing page with recent documents and the option to open other documents in the left pane. The main pane contains templates you can use to create a new document.

   c) Select the **Blank document** template.
      A new blank document opens with the **HOME** tab selected.

   d) Examine the groups on the **HOME** tab of the ribbon. Note that they include the **Clipboard**, **Font**, **Paragraph**, **Styles**, and **Editing** groups.

   e) Activate the tabs to the right of the **HOME** tab and explore the groups on each tab.

2. Open the **Font** dialog box.

   a) On the **HOME** tab, in the **Font** group, select the dialog box launcher.

   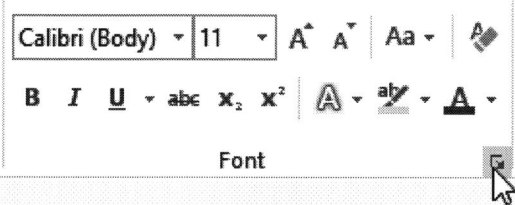

   b) Observe the available font formatting options.

   c) Select **Cancel** to close the dialog box.

3. Display the **Clipboard** task pane.

   a) On the **HOME** tab, in the **Clipboard** group, select the dialog box launcher.
      The **Clipboard** is currently empty.

   b) At the bottom of the **Clipboard** task pane, select **Options** to display options for the **Clipboard** task pane.
   c) Select the **Close** button on the task pane to close it.

4. Open the **Styles** gallery.

   a) In the **Styles** group, select the **More** button ⊡ to display a gallery of the styles available.

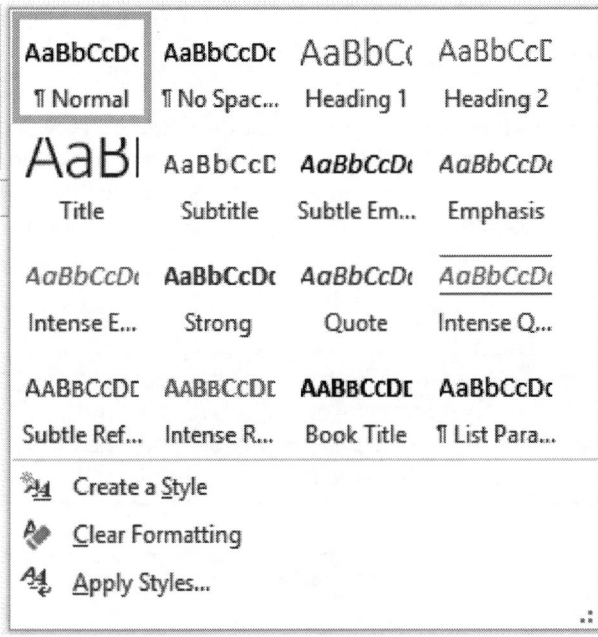

   b) Select anywhere within the document to close the **Styles** gallery.

5. Explore the **Backstage View**.
   a) Select the **FILE** tab.
   b) Observe the tabs available.
   c) In the right-hand pane, observe the information about **Document1**.

      The **Info** tab is active, and shows information about the current document, such as permissions and properties.
   d) Select the **Back** button to close the **Backstage View**.

6. Display ScreenTips for buttons on the **Quick Access Toolbar**.

   a) On the **Quick Access Toolbar**, position the mouse pointer over the **Save** button 🖫 to display its ScreenTip.
   b) Display the ScreenTip for the **Undo** button.

 **Note:** Since you haven't modified the document yet, there is nothing to undo.

# Document Views

A *document view* refers to a particular layout in which to view your document. This can be helpful when, for example, you'd like to see what your document would look like printed, or as an outline or a web page. The default document view is **Print Layout**. You can choose a different view by selecting the **VIEW** tab on the ribbon and choosing an option in the **Views** group. Alternatively, you can select any of the document view buttons on the status bar.

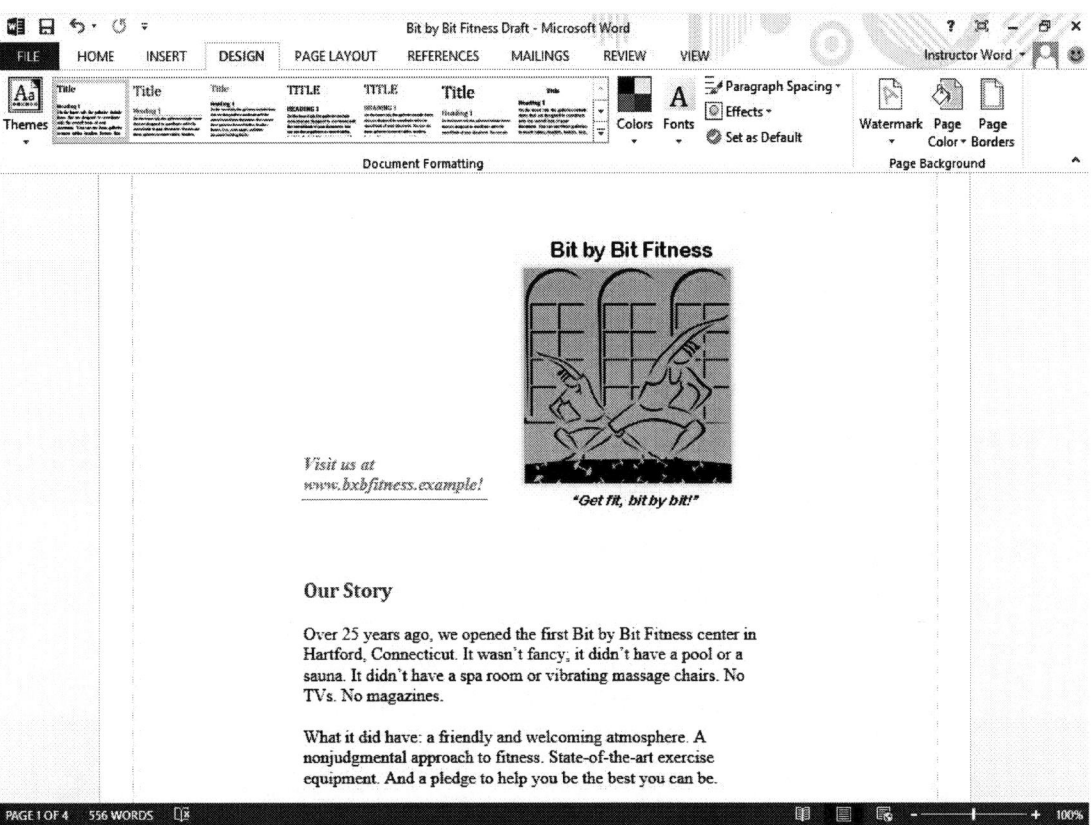

*Figure 1-7: A document in Print Layout view.*

Switching between document views is a common task when working with Word documents.

| View | Description |
|------|-------------|
| *Print Layout* | Shows the document as it will appear when printed. |
| *Read Mode* | Shows the document in read-only, full-screen mode in which the document is scrolled side to side rather than up and down. |
| *Web Layout* | Shows the document as it would appear in a web browser. |
| *Outline* | Shows the document data in a hierarchical mode, allowing you to insert and arrange topics and subtopics. |
| *Draft* | Shows the document without certain elements, such as graphics, or headers and footers. This view helps you quickly enter and edit text. |

Another type of view you are likely to encounter that isn't available from the **VIEW** menu is the **Protected** view. When you access a file that was created by someone other than yourself, a file you have downloaded from the Internet or other locations, the file is automatically opened in **Protected** view. This is a read-only view of the document designed to protect your computer from viruses. If you need to edit the file, select the **Enable Editing** button just below the Word menus.

If you were working on a document on one computer or device and open it on another computer or device, a bookmark indicates the location in the document where you were last working. Select the bookmark to jump to the last place you were working in the document.

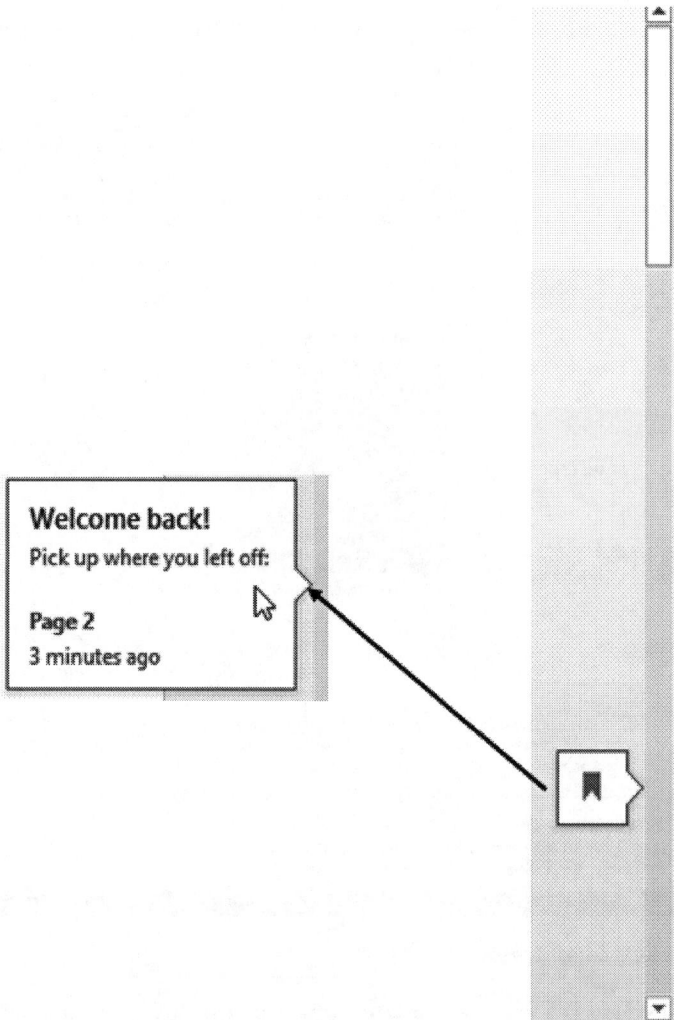

*Figure 1-8: A bookmark shows the last location where you were working in a document.*

 Access the Checklist tile on your LogicalCHOICE course screen for reference information and job aids on How to Open and Display a Document in Different Views

# ACTIVITY 1–2

## Opening and Displaying a Document in Different Views

### Data Files

C:\091024Data\Getting Started with Word\Bit by Bit Fitness Draft.docx

### Scenario

You know that you'll likely be working with many different types of documents. You might be writing content for the company's website, or you'll want to work in **Draft** view so that you can focus on writing rather than the layout of the page. You decide to experiment with different document views to get an idea of what your document will look like in various contexts.

1. Open **Bit by Bit Fitness Draft.docx**.
   a) Select **FILE→Open** to display the **Backstage** view.
   b) In the **Open** pane, select **Computer** and then select **Browse**.
   c) In the **Open** dialog box, browse to the **C:\091024Data\Getting Started with Word** folder.
   d) Select **Bit by Bit Fitness Draft.docx**.
   e) Select **Open**.

2. Display the document in different views.
   a) If the **Protected View** message appears across the top of the document, select **Enable Editing**.
   b) Select the **VIEW** tab.
   c) In the **Views** group, observe the highlighted view.
      The **Print Layout** button is highlighted. This is the default document view.
   d) In the **Views** group, select **Read Mode** to display the document in that view.
   e) Select **VIEW→Edit Document** to return to **Print Layout** view.
   f) On the status bar, select the **Web Layout** button to switch to **Web Layout** view.
   g) Using the **Views** group, switch to **Draft** view.
   h) Return the view to **Print Layout**.

## Window Views

*Window views* allow you to perform such tasks as moving between open documents, viewing documents side by side, or arranging multiple documents in a single window. You can access window views on the **VIEW** tab of the ribbon. Use the different window views to work with one or multiple documents.

| Option | Description |
| --- | --- |
| **New Window** | Opens the current document in a new window. |
| **Arrange All** | Tiles all open documents side by side on the screen. |
| **Split** | Splits the current window into two sections, allowing you to view different parts of the document at once. |

| Option | Description |
| --- | --- |
| **View Side by Side** | Displays two documents side by side. |
| **Synchronous Scrolling** | Allows you to scroll through side-by-side documents simultaneously. |
| **Reset Window Position** | Resets the position of the two documents being compared, so that each shares the screen equally. |
| **Switch Windows** | Switches between open documents. |

 **Access the Checklist tile on your LogicalCHOICE course screen for reference information and job aids on How to Apply Different Window Views**

# ACTIVITY 1-3
## Applying Different Window Views

### Data Files

C:\091024Data\Getting Started with Word\Newsletter content.docx

### Before You Begin

Bit by Bit Fitness Draft.docx is open.

### Scenario

It's possible that you'll need to view more than one document at a time in the course of your work, or that you'll want to see different sections of a document at once. You decide to get familiar with window views now, so that you'll know how to apply them when you need to later.

---

1. Select FILE→Open→Computer.

2. Under **Current Folder** select **C:\091024Data\Getting Started with Word**.

3. Select **Newsletter content.docx**. and select **Open**.

4. Switch to **Bit by Bit Fitness Draft.docx**.
   a) On the **VIEW** tab, in the **Window** group, select **Switch Windows** to display a list of open documents.
   b) From the list, select **Bit by Bit Fitness Draft.docx**.

5. View the documents side by side.
   a) On the **VIEW** tab, in the **Window** group, select **View Side by Side**.
   b) Scroll through one document to observe synchronous scrolling.
   c) Close **Newsletter content.docx**.

6. Split the window into two sections.
   a) On the **VIEW** tab, in the **Window** group, select **Split**.
   b) If necessary, drag the split toward the middle of the window to display the sections evenly.
   c) Scroll through both document sections.
   d) In the **Window** group, select **Remove Split**.

7. Open the document in a new window.
   a) In the **Window** group, select **New Window**.
   b) Switch windows to view the previous window, and then close it.

---

## Zoom Options

Word provides options to increase or decrease the magnification of your documents. You can access these options from the **Zoom** group on the **VIEW** tab, or from the status bar.

The zoom options are described in the following table.

| Option | Description |
| --- | --- |
| **Zoom** | Opens the **Zoom** dialog box, where you can select a preset or custom magnification level. |
| **100%** | Sets the magnification level to 100%. |
| **One Page** | Shows an entire page in the window. |
| **Multiple Pages** | Shows two or more pages side by side. |
| **Page Width** | Fits the page width to the width of the window. |
| **Zoom** slider | Lets you quickly adjust the magnification to a custom level. The **Zoom** slider is located on the status bar. |

 **Access the Checklist tile on your LogicalCHOICE course screen for reference information and job aids on How to Use Zoom Options in a Document**

## ACTIVITY 1-4
## Using Zoom Options

### Before You Begin
Bit by Bit Fitness Draft.docx is open.

### Scenario
As you continue to get acquainted with the Word interface, you know that you'll want to be able to inspect certain parts of your document close up, or perhaps get a "bird's-eye view" of those parts. You also want to set a magnification level that is comfortable for you to work with. You decide to experiment with different magnification levels.

1. Set magnification levels using the **Zoom** slider.
   a) On the **Zoom** slider, select the **Zoom In** button until the magnification level is 150 percent.

   b) Drag the **Zoom** slider until the magnification level is approximately 80 percent.

2. Set magnification levels using the **Zoom** group.
   a) On the **VIEW** tab, in the **Zoom** group, select **100%** to set the magnification to 100 percent.
   b) In the **Zoom** group, select the **Zoom** button to open the **Zoom** dialog box.
   c) Under **Zoom to**, select **75%**, and select **OK** to apply the new level.

3. Apply the magnification level of your choice.

      **Note:** Use any method you choose to change the magnification level.

# TOPIC B

## Create a Word Document

Now that you've become familiar with the Word application window, you can start to work with basic Word documents.

### Default Typing Options

Word sets certain default typing options that affect how text appears in your document. As you type, Word will automatically wrap text at the end of a line, check your spelling and grammar, and automatically correct certain typing errors. You can modify these options in the **Word Options** dialog box, accessible from the **FILE** tab.

- **Word Wrap**: Wraps a line of text to the beginning of the next line, eliminating the need for a manual return when you've reached the right-side margin.
- **AutoCorrect**: Corrects commonly misspelled words and typographical errors.
- **Check spelling as you type**: Word displays a wavy red line under text that Word considers a spelling error. You can right-click the word for a list of spelling suggestions.
- **Mark grammar errors as you type**: Word displays a wavy blue line under any text considered a grammar error. Right-clicking the text will display the grammar rule in question.

### The AutoCorrect Options Button

If you go back to a word corrected by **AutoCorrect**, a small button will appear under the word. If you select this button, Word gives you the option to change back to the original word, and stop automatically correcting it.

### On-screen Keyboard

If you are using a tablet, you also have the option of using the on-screen keyboard. Tap the screen with your finger or a stylus to display the on-screen keyboard. You can then use it to enter content into your Word document. You can connect a physical external keyboard to your tablet if you prefer not to use the on-screen keyboard.

### Formatting Marks

*Formatting marks* are nonprinting characters that display within the text to designate formatting elements such as spaces, tabs, and paragraph and line breaks. You can turn this display on or off by selecting the **Show/Hide ¶** button on the **HOME** tab.

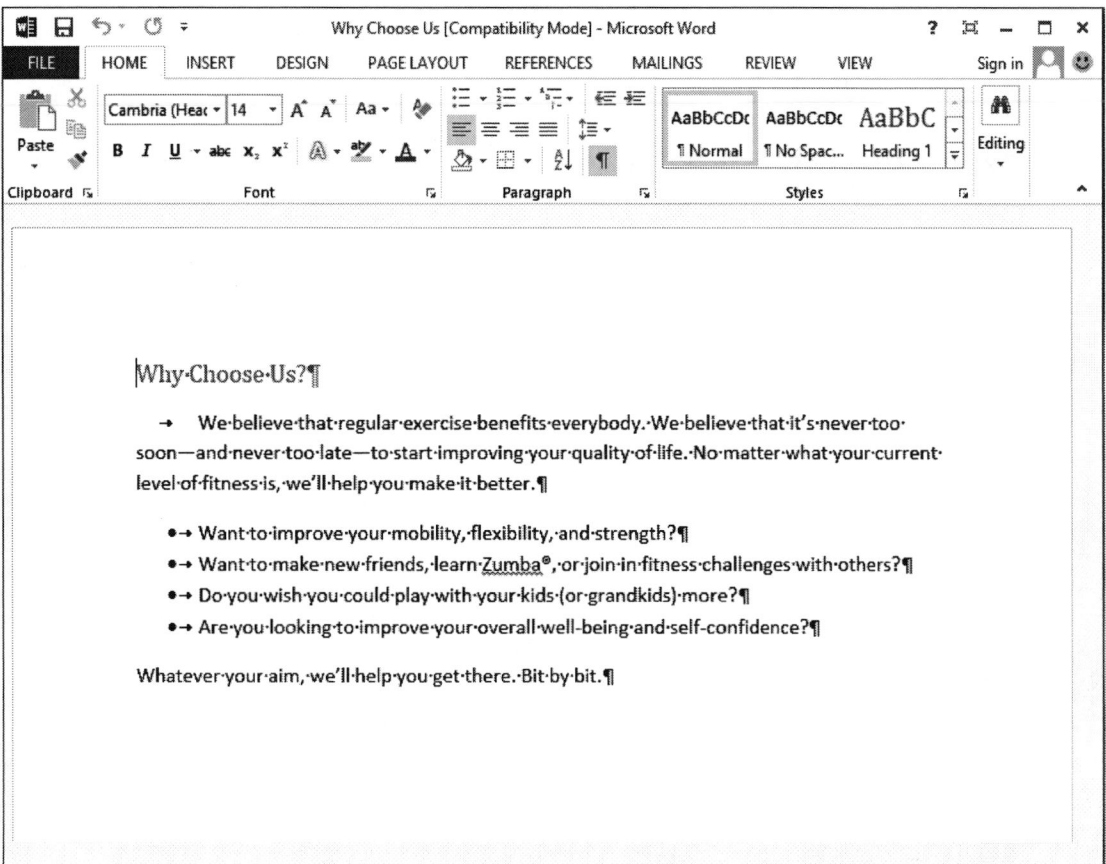

*Figure 1-9: Formatting marks displayed in a document.*

## Line Breaks

A *line break* is used to end a line before it wraps to the following line, but without starting a new paragraph. The advantage of using a line break in a paragraph is that the new line that follows the line break remains part of that paragraph and shares its properties. You can insert a line break by pressing **Shift+Enter**.

## Remove Blank Paragraphs

To make it easier to find blank paragraphs in your document that you want to remove, you can enable the **Show/Hide** feature to show the formatting marks. Select the ¶ and then press **Delete** to remove the blank paragraph.

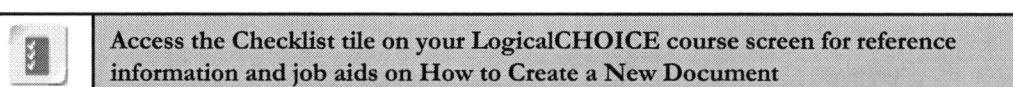

Access the Checklist tile on your LogicalCHOICE course screen for reference information and job aids on How to Create a New Document

Access the Checklist tile on your LogicalCHOICE course screen for reference information and job aids on How to Enter Text in a Document

# ACTIVITY 1-5
## Creating a New Document

### Before You Begin
Bit by Bit Fitness Draft.docx is open.

### Scenario
You think it's important to send a welcome letter to new members of Bit by Bit Fitness. Because one doesn't yet exist, you decide to create it.

1. Create a new document.
   a) On the **FILE** tab, select **New** to open the **Templates** gallery.
   b) In the gallery, select **Blank document** to create the new document.

2. Display formatting marks in the document.
   a) On the **HOME** tab, in the **Paragraph** group, select the **Show/Hide ¶** button.

3. Enter text.
   a) At the current insertion point, type *Welcome to Bit by Bit Fitness of Danbury!* and press **Enter**.
   b) Type *Our current monthly newsletter is enclosed. It's packed with fitness center information, our class schedule, event listings, and even a few recipes.*
   c) Observe that the text automatically wraps to the next line.

4. Replace the text "few recipes" with *recipe or two!*
   a) Press **Backspace** until the text is deleted, and then type the new text.

5. Verify that **AutoCorrect** is working.
   a) Press the **Spacebar** and type *Teh*
   b) Press the **Spacebar** again to allow **AutoCorrect** to correct the misspelled word to **The**.
   c) Position the mouse pointer below the corrected word to display the **AutoCorrect Options** button.

   d) Select the **AutoCorrect Options** button to display the options available for the misspelled word.
   e) Select **Control AutoCorrect Options** to open the **AutoCorrect: English (United States)** dialog box.
   f) Verify that the **Replace text as you type** box is checked.
   g) In the **Replace** text box, type *t*, then scroll down in the list to the entry "teh" to verify that it should be replaced with "the."

h) Select **OK** to close the dialog box.

## Save Options

The two basic options for saving a Word document are **Save** and **Save As**. You can access these options from the **FILE** tab. Additionally, the **Save** command appears as a button on the **Quick Access Toolbar**.

- **Save**: Saves a newly created document, or changes made to an existing document. When you save a document for the first time, the **Save As** dialog box opens. Here you'll name the document, choose the location in which to store it, and select its file type. The default file type of a Word 2013 document is .docx.
- **Save As**: Saves an existing document with a different name, location, or file type.

### Storage Locations

You can save your document to the local hard drive, a removable drive, a network drive, or to *SkyDrive*. SkyDrive is a Microsoft cloud service that enables you to access the files stored there from any device such as your office computer, home computer, smartphone, or tablet. SkyDrive is the default storage location for documents you save in Word.

### AutoSave

Word also provides the **AutoSave** feature, which operates in the background to automatically save your document at regular intervals. The default **AutoSave** interval is 10 minutes. You can configure **AutoSave** options in the **Word Options** dialog box.

 **Access the Checklist tile on your LogicalCHOICE course screen for reference information and job aids on How to Save a Basic Word Document**

## ACTIVITY 1-6
### Saving a Word Document

### Before You Begin

Bit by Bit Fitness Draft.docx is open.

Document2.docx is open.

### Scenario

Now that you've begun to create the welcome letter, you want to be sure you save it so that you can work on it later. You also want to save Bit by Bit Fitness Draft with another name, so that the original copy will remain unchanged.

1. Save Document2 for the first time.
   a) Select **FILE→Save** to display the **Save As** page.
   b) Select **Computer**.
   c) Under **Recent Folders** select **Getting Started with Word**. This is the C:\091024Data\Getting Started with Word folder.
   d) In the **File name** text box, type *My Welcome Letter*
   e) Observe that the default file type is **Word Document**.
   f) Select **Save**.

2. Quickly save changes to the document.
   a) In the document, delete the word **The** and then press **Enter** to insert a new blank line.
   b) Type *If you're new to a fitness regimen*
   c) On the **Quick Access Toolbar**, select the **Save** button 💾 to save the changes you made to the document.
   d) Close **My Welcome Letter**.

3. Save Bit by Bit Fitness Draft with a different file name.
   a) Select **FILE→Save As** to open the **Save As** page.
   b) In the right pane under **Computer→Current Folder**, select **Getting Started with Word**.
   c) In the **File name** text box, change the name to *My Bit by Bit Fitness Draft*
   d) Select **Save**.

### Preview and Print Options

Depending on the type of document you've created, you may want to print it eventually. It's important to preview the document before printing it, in order to identify obvious formatting errors and to verify that all the elements are where you want them. To preview a document, on the **FILE** tab, select the **Print** tab. The document preview appears in a large pane to the right of the print options.

Once you've verified the preview, you can choose from among several print options.

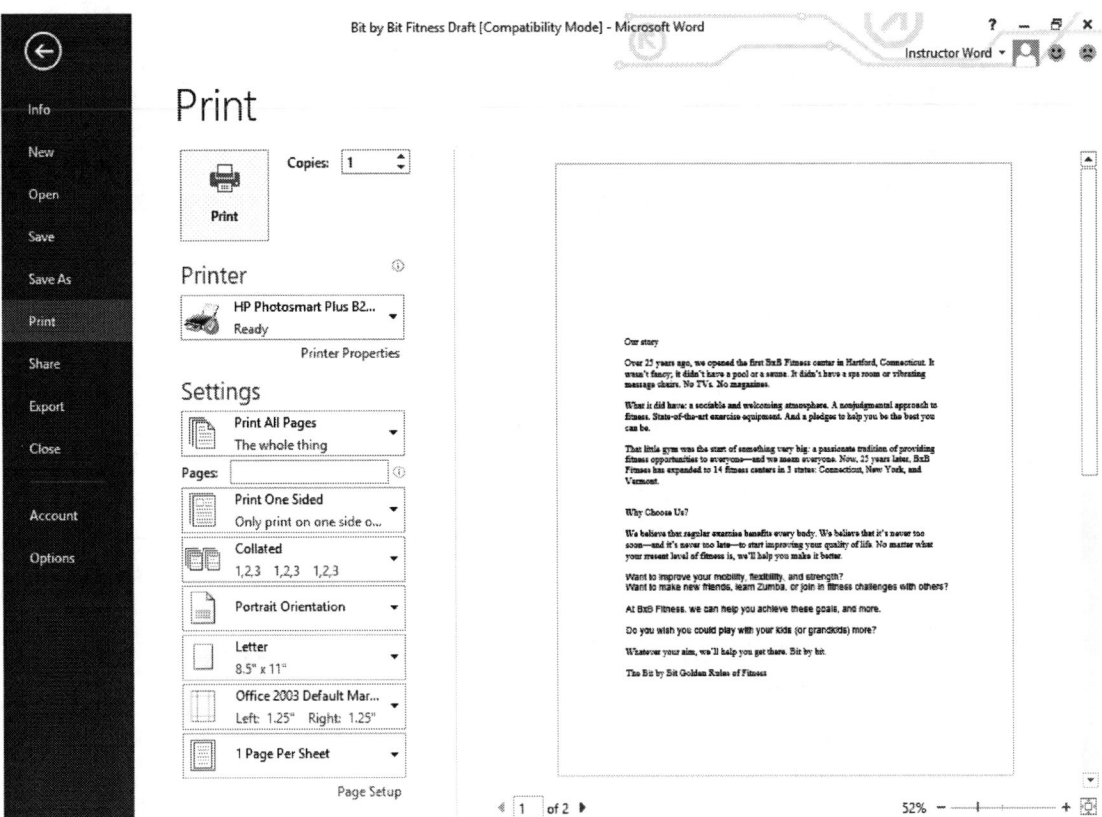

*Figure 1-10: The Print window.*

You'll see three sections on the **Print** tab:

- **Print**: Sends the document to the printer. Additionally, you can select the number of copies to be printed.
- **Printer**: Identifies the default printer. You can select a different printer from the drop-down list.
- **Settings**: Shows optional settings to apply before sending the document to the printer. Here, you can select the paper size, change the page orientation and margins, and so on. You can also open the **Page Setup** dialog box.

 Access the Checklist tile on your LogicalCHOICE course screen for reference information and job aids on **How to Preview and Print a Document**

# ACTIVITY 1-7
## Previewing and Printing a Document

### Before You Begin
My Bit by Bit Fitness Draft.docx is open.

### Scenario
You want to print out two copies of My Bit by Bit Fitness Draft, so that you and your manager can look over the document together. You decide that you'd like to preview the document before printing it to verify that it contains no obvious formatting problems.

---

1. Preview the document.
   a) Select FILE→Print.
   b) In the **Preview** pane, at the bottom center of the window, select the **Next Page** button to preview the second page of the document.

   c) Using the **Zoom** slider, decrease the magnification level so that both pages are displayed.

2. Print the document.
   a) In the **Copies** spin box, click the up arrow once to set the number of copies to **2**.
   b) Select the **Print** button to print two copies of the document.

---

# TOPIC C

# Help

When you're first learning about the features of an application, you'll understandably have many questions. In this topic, you'll use the Help feature in Word to find answers to your questions.

## Help Options

*Word Help* is a repository of information about the various tools and features of Word. With **Word Help**, you can find answers to Word-related questions quickly and easily. You can access **Word Help** from the **Microsoft Word Help (F1)** button on the ribbon, or you can press **F1**.

When you first open the **Word Help** window, you'll see a toolbar, a **Search** box, a **Search** button, and a **Search Results** pane, where the results of your searches will appear.

The default search scope for **Word Help** connects you to Office.com. You can narrow the search scope to information local to your personal computer.

| Component | Description |
|---|---|
| **Search** text box | Allows you to enter a keyword to search for. |
| **Search** button | Performs the keyword search. You can also select the drop-down arrow here to choose a search scope. |
| **Search Results** pane | Shows the results of your search. Initially, it displays Help topics you can browse through. |

You can use the buttons on the toolbar to perform several different tasks while in **Word Help**.

| Button | Function |
|---|---|
| **Back** | Moves back one screen. |
| **Forward** | Moves forward one screen. |
| **Home** | Displays the **Home** page of Word Help. |
| **Print** | Prints the contents of the **Search Results** pane. |
| **Use Large Text** | Changes the font size of the **Search Results** pane contents. |
| **Keep Help on Top (Ctrl + T)** | Pins the **Word Help** window so that it remains open on top of any other open windows. |

 **Access the Checklist tile on your LogicalCHOICE course screen for reference information and job aids on How to Find Help**

# ACTIVITY 1-8
## Finding Help in Word

### Before You Begin

My Bit by Bit Fitness Draft.docx is open.

### Scenario

You'd like more information about printing Word documents. You may need to know how to print on both sides of a sheet of paper, or how to apply other options when printing a document. You'd also like to look at additional information about Word basics. You decide to use the Word Help feature to find answers to your questions.

---

1. Open the **Word Help** window.
   a) Select the **Microsoft Word Help (F1)** button on the ribbon.

2. Perform a keyword search for "printing."
   a) In the **Word Help** window, in the **Search** text box, type *printing*
   b) Select the **Search** button to start the search.

   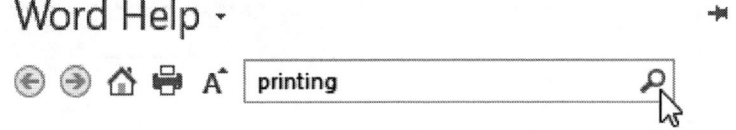

   c) In the **Search Results** pane, select **Print and preview documents** to open the article.
   d) Read the information about printing in Word.
   e) On the **Word Help** toolbar, select the **Back** button to go back to the search results.

3. View **Word Help** topics on the **Home** page.

    **Note:** If you are using a tablet, select the **Touch Guide** link for information on the gestures to use in Word.

   a) On the toolbar, select the **Home** button.

Word Help ˅

b) Select **Learn Word basics**.

c) Scroll through the article to see some of the kinds of information available in the article.

4. Close the **Word Help** window.

5. Select **FILE→Close** to close **My Bit by Bit Fitness Draft.docx**.

# Summary

In this lesson, you identified some of the fundamental tools and features of Word 2013, and began to work with Word documents. You examined components of the Word application window; opened a document and applied different views to it; and created, saved, and printed a document. You also used the **Word Help** feature to find information about a specific Word topic. Becoming familiar with these basic functions prepares you to perform more complex tasks in Word.

**What will you use Word 2013 for in your workplace?**

**How do the default typing options in Word help you when creating documents?**

 **Note:** Check your LogicalCHOICE Course screen for opportunities to interact with your classmates, peers, and the larger LogicalCHOICE online community about the topics covered in this course or other topics you are interested in. From the Course screen you can also access available resources for a more continuous learning experience.

# 2 Editing a Document

**Lesson Time: 1 hour**

## Lesson Objectives

In this lesson, you will:

- Navigate through a document to find and select text.
- Modify selected text.
- Find and replace text.

## Lesson Introduction

You've examined the Microsoft® Word 2013 interface, and created your first document. It's typical for a document to undergo many changes before it's finalized. You'll often want to add more text, or delete text from your document. You may want to cut text, copy text from one document and paste it in another, or replace text. These fundamental techniques will help you get started with editing text in your documents.

# TOPIC A

## Navigate and Select Text

Once you've created and saved a Word document, you may find that some of the text in it isn't quite what you want, so you'll make some editing changes. When editing, it's handy to be able to move quickly through a document to find and select the text you want to change. Using appropriate navigation techniques will help you locate the text you want. Word provides various interface components for navigating through a document.

## Scroll Bars

You can use the scroll bars in the Word application window to navigate through a document. The horizontal scroll bar appears at the bottom of the window, just above the status bar, and allows you to scroll from left to right. The vertical scroll bar is located to the right of the document area, and allows you to move up or down within the document. You can use the arrows at the ends of either scroll bar to scroll incrementally through the document, or you can drag the slider within the scroll bar to navigate the document more quickly.

## Keyboard Navigation

In addition to using the scroll bars, you can move through a document using navigation keys on the keyboard. You can use navigation keys to move the insertion point by one character, a word, a line, a paragraph, or to the beginning or end of a document.

## Text Selection

You can select text in a document by using the mouse, the keyboard, or a combination of both. You can select characters individually by highlighting them, or you can select entire paragraphs by simply clicking on any position within that paragraph. In addition, you can use the *selection bar*. The selection bar is a region on the left margin of a document that is used to select text. When you position the mouse pointer in the selection bar, the pointer changes from an I-beam to a right-pointing arrow. With the mouse pointer in the selection bar, you can then click to select and highlight a line, double-click to select and highlight a paragraph, or triple-click to select and highlight all content in the document.

You may decide to delete the text you've selected. If so, simply press **Delete**.

### Mini Toolbar

When text is selected, the **Mini** toolbar is displayed. It contains a subset of the commands available on the ribbon in an easily accessible **Mini** toolbar adjacent to the selected text.

 **Access the Checklist tile on your LogicalCHOICE course screen for reference information and job aids on How to Navigate and Select Text**

# ACTIVITY 2-1
## Navigating and Selecting Text

### Data Files

C:\091024Data\Editing a Document\Bit by Bit Fitness Draft.docx

### Scenario

You want to look through the Bit by Bit Fitness draft document so that you can start thinking about ways to improve it. You decide to navigate through the document first, to familiarize yourself with its content, and practice various selection techniques that will help you with future editing tasks.

---

1. From the C:\091024Data\Editing a Document folder, open **Bit by Bit Fitness Draft.docx**.
   a) Select **FILE→Open**.
   b) Select **Computer**.
   c) Select **Browse**.
   d) Navigate to the **C:\091024Data\Editing a Document** folder.
   e) Select **Bit by Bit Fitness Draft.docx**.
   f) Select **Open**.

2. Save the document in the current folder as *My Bit by Bit Fitness Draft.docx*
   a) Select **FILE→Save As**.
   b) Select **Computer**.
   c) Under **Current Folder**, select **Editing a Document**.
   d) In the **File name** text box, position the insertion point to the left of the current file name.
   e) Type *My* to name the file "My Bit by Bit Fitness Draft.docx."
   f) Select **Save**.

3. On the vertical scroll bar, click the bottom arrow repeatedly to scroll until the first paragraph under **Why Choose Us?** is visible.

4. Use the selection bar to select the paragraph.
   a) Place the mouse pointer in the blank area to the left of the first paragraph under **Why Choose Us?**.
   b) Click and drag the pointer to select the text, or double-click to make the selection.
      The **Mini** toolbar is displayed when text is selected.
   c) Click an area away from the selection to deselect the text.

5. Select text in the paragraph.
   a) In the paragraph, double-click the word "believe" to select it.
   b) Deselect the word.

6. Use the keyboard to navigate to the beginning of the next page.
   a) Press **Ctrl+Page Down**.

7. On the second page, under **What We Offer**, select the text "Bite by Bite Café."

    **Note:** You could click before the **B**, then press **Ctrl+Shift+Right Arrow** to select the text. Hold down the **Ctrl+Shift** and press **Right Arrow** four times.

   a) Click to the left of the first B in "Bite by Bite Café."

      b)  Drag across the text "Bite by Bite Café."

8.  Press **Ctrl+Home** to navigate to the beginning of the document.

9.  Select all the text in the document.

      a)  Press **Ctrl+A**.

      b)  Click anywhere in the document to deselect the text.

# TOPIC B

## Modify Text

Once you've located and selected the text you're looking for, you might want to change it in some way. Maybe you want to move the text to another place in the document where it fits better, or copy the text so that it appears in more than one location in the document. You might want to copy information from one document verbatim into another document. Word helps you accomplish these editing tasks quickly.

## The Clipboard Task Pane

The **Clipboard** task pane displays items on the *clipboard*, which is a temporary storage area for content that has been cut or copied from a document. The clipboard can store up to 24 items, and you can transfer items from the clipboard to another place in the document, or to a different document, using the **Paste** command.

When you copy content to the clipboard, the latest items appear at the top of the **Clipboard** task pane. You can use the **Clipboard** task pane to paste objects, clear all objects from the clipboard, and customize the task pane.

There are several customization options for the **Clipboard** task pane, which you can access from the **Options** button at the bottom of the pane.

| Option | Description |
|---|---|
| **Show Office Clipboard Automatically** | Displays the **Clipboard** task pane whenever you open a document. |
| **Show Office Clipboard When Ctrl+C Pressed Twice** | Opens the task pane using the keyboard. |
| **Collect Without Showing Office Clipboard** | Collects items to the clipboard without displaying the task pane. |
| **Show Office Clipboard Icon on Taskbar** | Displays the **Office Clipboard** icon on the taskbar. |
| **Show Status Near Taskbar When Copying** | Displays an informational message above the **Office Clipboard** icon about the item being copied. |

## Text Editing Options

There are various methods in Word that you can use to move a selection of text from one location to another, either within the same document, or to a different document.

| Method | Description |
|---|---|
| Cut and paste | After selecting text, you can choose to cut it from the document and move it to the clipboard, to be pasted in another location, if needed. |
| Drag | After selecting text, you can drag it to the desired location. The drag method does not place the content on the clipboard. |
| Copy and paste | After selecting text, you can copy it to the clipboard and paste it in a new location. The original selection remains in its current location. |

## Paste Options

You have several options when pasting selections that you have cut or copied in a document. On the **HOME** tab, in the **Clipboard** group, the **Paste** button has several options:

- **Keep Source Formatting**: Preserve the original formatting of the text.
- **Merge Formatting**: Use the formatting of the new location.
- **Keep Text Only**: Discard the formatting from both source and destination, and paste the selection as plain text.
- **Paste Special**: Opens the **Paste Special** dialog box, where you can specify the format of the pasted text.
- **Set Default Paste**: Opens the **Word Options** dialog box, where you can change the default pasting options, such as how to format the pasted text.

If you just click the **Paste** button, the default paste type is to keep source formatting.

### The Paste Options Button

The **Paste Options** button appears after an item is pasted, and selecting it displays a menu of formatting choices for the pasted content. The choices available will depend on the source of the content. The options are **Keep Source Formatting**, **Merge Formatting**, and **Keep Text Only**.

## Live Preview

The *Live Preview* feature allows you to preview certain formatting changes to your document before you actually apply them. This helps you decide whether the new formatting is appropriate or desirable. For example, when you select text and point to a formatting style on the ribbon, **Live Preview** will display the text as it would appear with the new style.

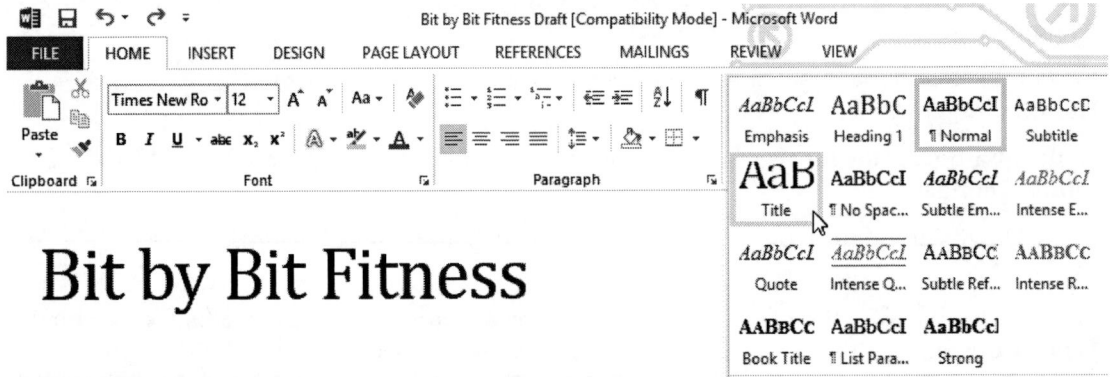

*Figure 2–1: Displaying a formatting style in Live Preview.*

### Preview Paste Options

**Live Preview** also allows you to see the result of a paste operation before you carry it out. When you place the insertion point in the location where you want to paste content and then point to one of the individual paste options available, Word will display a preview of the text with that option applied.

 **Note:** If **Paste Live Preview** isn't working, go to **Options→Advanced→Editing Options→Use smart selection.**

 Access the **Checklist** tile on your **LogicalCHOICE** course screen for reference information and job aids on How to Copy and Paste Text

# ACTIVITY 2-2
## Copying and Pasting Text

### Before You Begin
My Bit by Bit Fitness Draft.docx is open.

### Scenario
Now that you've had a chance to become familiar with the information in the Bit by Bit Fitness draft document, you see that much of it is intended for use as promotional material for the company. It would probably be a good idea to put some contact information at the very beginning, so that when the document is in its final form, a reader will know immediately where to go for more information. You decide to copy and paste the web address at the beginning of the document.

1. Copy the sentence containing the website address from the end of the document.
   a) Press **Ctrl+End** to move to the end of the document.
   b) Select the sentence "Visit us at www.bxbfitness.example!"
   c) On the **HOME** tab, in the **Clipboard** group, select **Copy**, or press **Ctrl+C**.

2. Paste the sentence above the "Our story" section at the beginning of the document.
   a) Navigate to the beginning of the document and place the insertion point two lines above "Our story."
      If paragraph marks are not displayed, select **Home→Show/Hide ¶** to make it easier to see where the paste the text.
   b) On the **HOME** tab, in the **Clipboard** group, select **Paste**, or press **Ctrl+V**.
   c) If necessary, ensure that there is a blank line between the pasted text and "Our story."

3. Save your changes.

## The Undo Command

The **Undo** command will correct unintended or erroneous actions immediately after they are made. For example, you may have pasted text in the wrong spot in your document, or mistakenly deleted text. If you use the **Undo** command right away, you can undo those actions. You can execute the **Undo** command by selecting the **Undo** button on the **Quick Access Toolbar**, or by pressing **Ctrl +Z**.

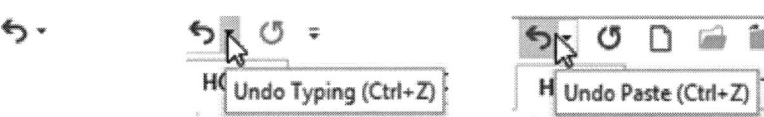

*Figure 2-2: The ScreenTip for Undo changes based on the last action taken.*

## The Redo Command

The **Redo** button on the **Quick Access Toolbar** allows you to redo an action that you just executed, such as a paste operation or even a sentence you typed. The **Redo** command works only for the current working session. Once you close a document, the **Redo** list is cleared. You can execute the **Redo** command by selecting the **Redo** button on the **Quick Access Toolbar**, or by pressing **Ctrl+Y**.

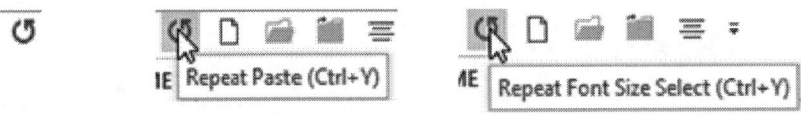

*Figure 2–3: The Redo command ScreenTip changes based on the last action taken.*

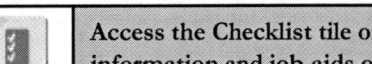 Access the Checklist tile on your LogicalCHOICE course screen for reference information and job aids on How to Use the Undo and Redo Commands

# ACTIVITY 2-3
## Using the Undo and Redo Commands

### Before You Begin
My Bit by Bit Fitness Draft.docx is open.

### Scenario
You've found a section in the document that you don't think is useful, so you decide to delete it to see how the document reads without it. If you change your mind, you can quickly insert the text again.

---

1.  Delete some text.
    a)  On the first page of the document, select the line "At BxB Fitness, we can help you achieve these goals, and more."
    b)  Press **Delete**.

2.  Use **Redo** to delete a blank line.
    a)  On the **Quick Access Toolbar**, select the **Redo** button to repeat the last action taken.

    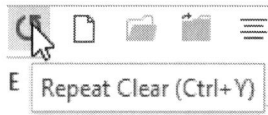

    The ScreenTip indicates that the action taken will be **Repeat Clear**.
    b)  Select **Redo** two more times to delete additional text.

3.  Undo the deletions.
    a)  On the **Quick Access Toolbar**, select the **Undo** button. The last item you deleted is restored.

    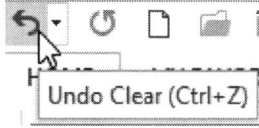

    b)  Select **Undo** until all of the text you deleted is restored.

4.  Save your changes.

---

# TOPIC C

## Find and Replace Text

A common editing task involves replacing certain words or phrases. You can manually search for the text you want to replace, but in large documents, this can be a daunting and time-consuming task. Fortunately, Word 2013 provides methods for making such a task speedier and much more efficient.

### The Navigation Pane

On the **HOME** tab, in the **Editing** group, select the **Find** button, or press **Ctrl+F**, to open the **Navigation** pane. To find a specific word or phrase in your document, type it into the **Search document** text box. Word then highlights all instances of the search term, and lists them in the pane. The **Navigation** pane also contains tabbed navigation options, which allow you to choose how you want to browse the results of your search. The **HEADINGS** tab is the default option, but you can also choose to browse the results by pages or results in the document.

Select the down arrow in the **Search document** text box to display the **Search for more things** menu if you want to specify other search options in the **Navigation** pane. From this menu, you can set the search options, perform an advanced find, replace text, and go directly to a specific location in the document. You can also search for graphics, tables, equations, footnotes or endnotes, and comments.

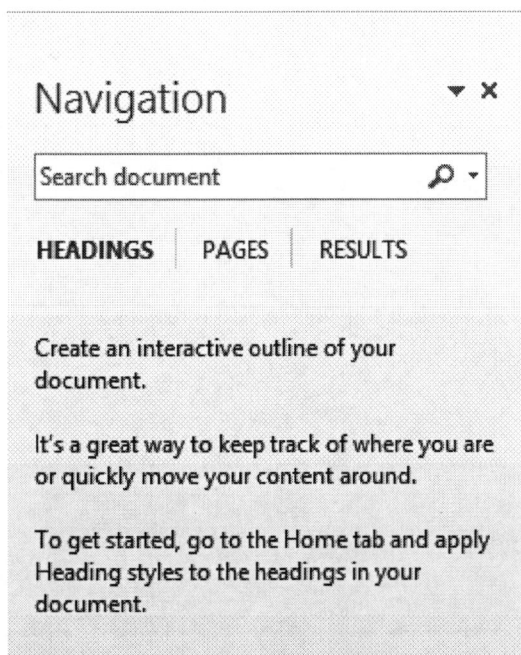

*Figure 2–4: The Navigation pane.*

## The Find and Replace Dialog Box

You can use the **Find and Replace** dialog box to find text, replace text, or go to a specific location in your document.

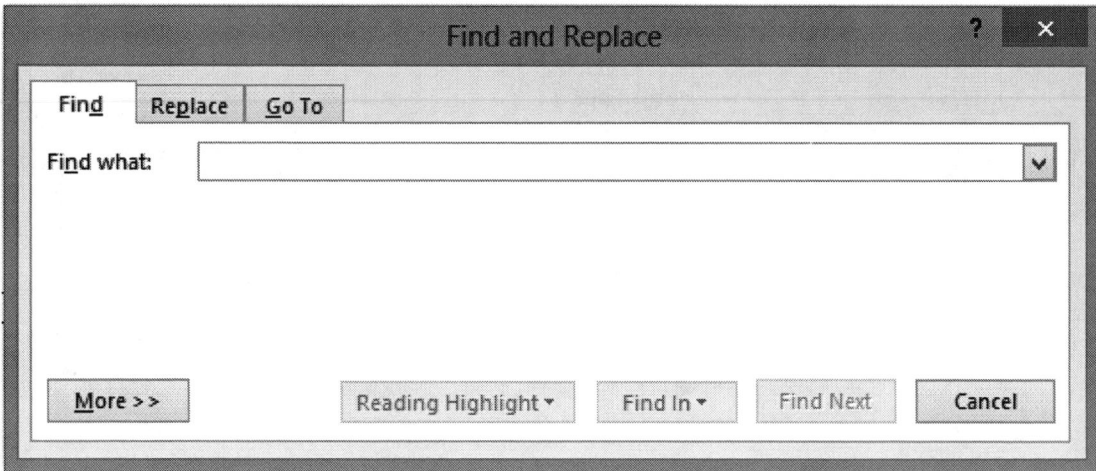

*Figure 2-5: The Find and Replace dialog box.*

Each tab in the **Find and Replace** dialog box contains additional options for finding and replacing text.

| Tab | Description |
| --- | --- |
| Find | Provides options for specifying the search criteria. |
| Replace | Provides options for replacing found text. You can press **Ctrl+H** to display the **Find and Replace** dialog box with the **Replace** tab selected. |
| Go To | Provides options for specifying a location in the document you want to navigate to. You can press **Ctrl+G** to display the **Find and Replace** dialog box with the **Go To** tab selected. |

## Find Options

Find options are an extension of the **Find and Replace** dialog box. Using these options, you can modify the search behavior of the **Find** command in Word. The **Find Options** dialog box contains an assortment of options to fine-tune your search criteria, such as matching case, or finding only whole words. In the **Navigation** pane, you can access the **Find Options** dialog box by selecting the down arrow in the **Search document** text box and selecting **Options** from the menu.

The options are also accessible from the **Find and Replace** dialog box. Select **More>>** to display the **Search Options** section of the dialog box.

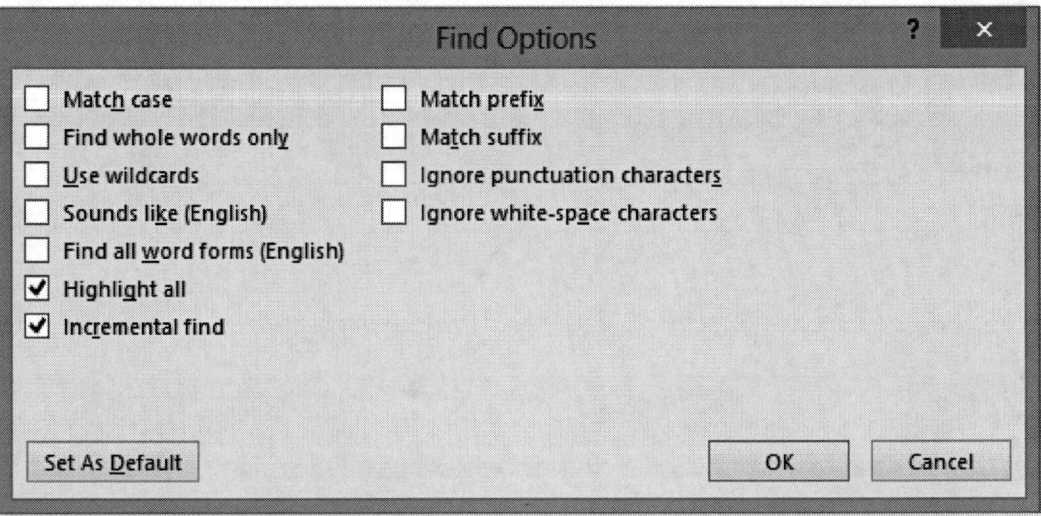

*Figure 2–6: The Find Options dialog box.*

## Find and Replace with Wildcards

You can use wildcards in the **Find and Replace** dialog box. This can be useful if you are searching for text that begins or ends with certain characters, or for finding things like multiple characters. When the use of wildcards is enabled, the **Match case** and **Find whole words only** options are disabled. There are several wildcards you can use with find and replace.

| Wildcard | Used to Find | Example | Example Results |
|---|---|---|---|
| ? | Any single character | we?k | week, weak, welk |
| * | Any string of characters | we* | we, week, weak, welcome, weeds |
| < | Characters at the beginning of a word | <(red) | red, redden, redeem; *does not find* kindred, blurred |
| > | Characters at the end of a word | (ing)> | blurring, weeding, sing; *does not find* finger, winged |
| [x-z] | Any single character within the specified range | [a-z]ing | ding, ring, zing; *does not find* bring |
| [!x-z] | Any single character *except* the characters within the specified range | sw[!a-i]m | swum; *does not find* swam, swim |
| {n} | Specified number of occurrences of the previous character or expression | che{2}p | cheep; *does not find* cheap, cheeep |
| {n,} | At least the specified number of occurrences of the previous character or expression | hop{1,}ed | hoped, hopped |
| {n,m} | From *n* to *m* occurrences of the previous character or expression | 101{1,4} | 101, 1011, 10111, 101111; *does not find* 1001, 10101010, 1011111 |
| @ | One or more occurrences of the previous character or expression | ho@p | hop, hoop, hoooooop |

| Wildcard | Used to Find | Example | Example Results |
|---|---|---|---|
| \ | A character that is one of the defined wildcard characters | \? | ? |
| | | \* | * |
| | | \@ | @ |

## Combining Wildcards

You can combine wildcards to create more complex searches. You can also add parentheses around wildcards and text to specify the order in which the items are evaluated. For example, <(un)*(ing)> would find any words that begin with "un" and end with "ing" and contain any characters in between.

## Changing Word Positions

If you need to change the position of two words throughout your document, you can specify the words in the **Find** text box, then in the **Replace** text box, type \2 \1. For example (Washington) (George) in the **Find** text box and \2 \1 in the **Replace** text box, would replace Washington George with George Washington.

 **Access the Checklist tile on your LogicalCHOICE course screen for reference information and job aids on How to Find and Replace Text**

# ACTIVITY 2–4
## Finding and Replacing Text

### Before You Begin
My Bit by Bit Fitness Draft.docx is open.

### Scenario
You've noticed that the word "fitness" appears frequently in the document. At some point, you may want to replace it with an alternative, but for now, you'd just like to know the number of occurrences of the word. Similarly, it appears that the original author of the document used an abbreviated word for the name of the company, rather than typing it out completely. You decide to replace the abbreviation with the full company name. You want to be sure, however, that you don't replace the text in the web address.

1. Find the number of instances of the word "fitness."
   a) Place the insertion point at the beginning of the document.
   b) On the **HOME** tab, in the **Editing** group, select **Find** to open the **Navigation** task pane.
   c) If necessary, select **RESULTS**.

   d) In the **Search document** text box, type *fitness*
      The **Navigation** pane shows the number of matches, and a list of all the instances of the word.
   e) Close the **Navigation** task pane.

2. Replace "BxB" with "Bit by Bit."
   a) On the **HOME** tab, in the **Editing** group, select **Replace** to open the **Find and Replace** dialog box.
   b) On the **Replace** tab, in the **Find what** text box, type *BxB*
   c) In the **Replace with** text box, type *Bit by Bit*
   d) If necessary, select the **More** button to expand the search options.
   e) Under **Search Options**, check **Match case**.
   f) Select **Find Next** to find the first occurrence of "BxB."
   g) Select **Replace** to replace the term, and move to the next occurrence.
   h) Select **Replace All** to replace the remaining instances of the term.
   i) Select **OK** to close the message box.
   j) Close the dialog box, and verify that the text was changed.

3. Save your changes, and close the document.

# Summary

In this lesson, you used various methods to change text in your document. You navigated through a document and selected text, copied and pasted text, and used the **Navigation** pane to find text. It's important to be able to move text around in a document, and quickly find and replace text with minimal effort. These foundational skills will assist you in easily and efficiently editing your Word documents.

**What Word components do you think you'll use most often when searching for and editing text in your documents?**

**In what way will the editing techniques in Word help you work more effectively?**

 **Note:** Check your LogicalCHOICE Course screen for opportunities to interact with your classmates, peers, and the larger LogicalCHOICE online community about the topics covered in this course or other topics you are interested in. From the Course screen you can also access available resources for a more continuous learning experience.

# 3 | Formatting Text and Paragraphs

**Lesson Time: 1 hour, 30 minutes**

## Lesson Objectives

In this lesson, you will:

- Apply character formatting options to text.
- Align paragraphs in a document using tab stops.
- Display text as list items.
- Control paragraph layout.
- Apply borders and shading to paragraphs.
- Apply styles to text in a document.
- Manage formatting in a document.

## Lesson Introduction

Once you've learned how to perform basic editing techniques, you'll often want to make further changes to the appearance of text and paragraphs. A document is more visually appealing—and more readable—when certain formatting and layout options are applied. In this lesson, you'll learn some basic techniques for enhancing the appearance of your documents.

# TOPIC A

## Apply Character Formatting

To help certain text elements stand out in your document, you can apply various formatting options, such as different font styles or highlighting. You may find that you like the formatting of certain text and want to apply it to other text selections. Word provides a number of character formatting techniques to improve and emphasize the appearance of text in your documents.

### Fonts

A *font* is a set of characters with a specific style and size. The character set in a font includes letters, numbers, and punctuation marks.

A document can have more than one font applied to the text it contains. Word supplies a number of font choices to suit almost any purpose, and makes it easy to apply different font styles and sizes.

| | | |
|---|---|---|
| Calibri 12 pt | Calibri 16 pt | **Bold Text Style** |
| Times New Roman 12 pt | Times New Roman 16 pt | *Italicized Text Style* |
| Arial 12 pt | Arial 16 pt | <u>Underline Text Style</u> |

*Figure 3-1: Text with different fonts applied.*

### The Mini Toolbar

The *Mini toolbar* is a floating toolbar that appears when you select text in a document. It displays options to format the selection without having to work with tabs on the ribbon. When you move the mouse pointer away from the selected text, the toolbar disappears.

You can also invoke the **Mini** toolbar, along with a menu of other commands, by right-clicking anywhere in the document.

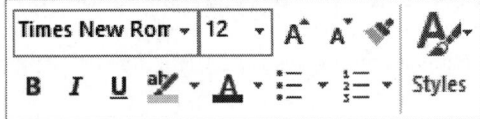

*Figure 3-2: The Mini toolbar.*

### Font Options

In Word, you have a multitude of choices for changing the appearance of a font. You can change the style, size, and color. You can apply different emphasis properties and effects, and change the case. You can apply these options from the **Mini** toolbar, by using the **Font** group on the **HOME** tab, or by using the **Font** dialog box.

Word includes four font styles.

| Style | Description |
|---|---|
| **Bold** | Applies bold formatting to the text. |
| **Italic** | Italicizes the text. |
| **Bold Italic** | Bolds and italicizes the text. |
| **Underline** | Underlines the text. |

In addition to specifying a particular font size, you can quickly increase or decrease font size.

| Option | Description |
|---|---|
| **Increase Font Size** | Increases the font size by one point each time you select it. |
| **Decrease Font Size** | Decreases the font size by one point each time you select it. |

Word provides several effects you can apply to text.

| Effect | Description |
|---|---|
| **Strikethrough** | Runs a line through the selected text. This effect is conventionally used to denote information that was deleted. |
| **Double strikethrough** | Runs two lines through the selected text. This effect is used when more emphasis is needed than what is provided by a single strikethrough. |
| **Subscript** | Decreases the font size and moves the text below the text baseline. |
| **Superscript** | Decreases the font size and moves the text above the text line. |
| **Small caps** | Converts all the characters in the selected text to uppercase, but reduces them to dimensions similar to lowercase characters. However, any capital letters converted to small caps will be slightly larger than the rest of the letters. |
| **All caps** | Capitalizes all the characters of the selected text, resulting in all the characters being the same size. |
| **Hidden** | Hides the selected text. |

You can apply different case options to text.

| Option | Description |
|---|---|
| **Sentence case** | Capitalizes the first letter of every sentence in the selected text. |
| **lowercase** | Converts all the characters of the selected text into small letters. |
| **UPPERCASE** | Capitalizes all the characters of the selected text. |
| **Capitalize Each Word** | Capitalizes the first letter of each word in the selected text. |
| **tOGGLE cASE** | Inverts the current capitalization of the selection. Lowercase letters become uppercase, and vice versa. |

## Keyboard Shortcuts for Font Styles

You can press key combinations to quickly apply font styles. For example, press **Ctrl+B** to apply bold formatting, and press **Ctrl+I** to italicize the selected text.

**Note:** To further learn about shortcuts, you can access the LearnTO **Save Time with Keyboard Shortcuts** presentation from the **LearnTO** tile on the LogicalCHOICE Course screen.

**Access the Checklist tile on your LogicalCHOICE course screen for reference information and job aids on How to Apply Different Font Options**

# ACTIVITY 3-1

## Applying Different Font Options to Text

### Data Files

C:\091024Data\Formatting Text and Paragraphs\Bit by Bit Fitness Draft.docx

### Scenario

You've noticed that there are two different fonts in the document, and the effect is rather jarring. You'd like all the text to be in the same Candara, 12 point font. Additionally, you want to format some text so that it stands out more from the rest of the content. You decide to begin by applying new font options to the first heading in the document.

---

1. In the C:\091024Data\Formatting Text and Paragraphs folder, open **Bit by Bit Fitness Draft.docx**, and save it as *My Bit by Bit Fitness Draft.docx* in the current folder.

2. Format all the text with the Candara, 12 point size.

   a) Select all the text.

    **Caution:** Be careful not to press any keys while the text is selected, as this will delete all the text. If this happens, select the **Undo** button.

   b) On the **HOME** tab, in the **Font** group, in the **Font** box, select the arrow to display the **Font** gallery.

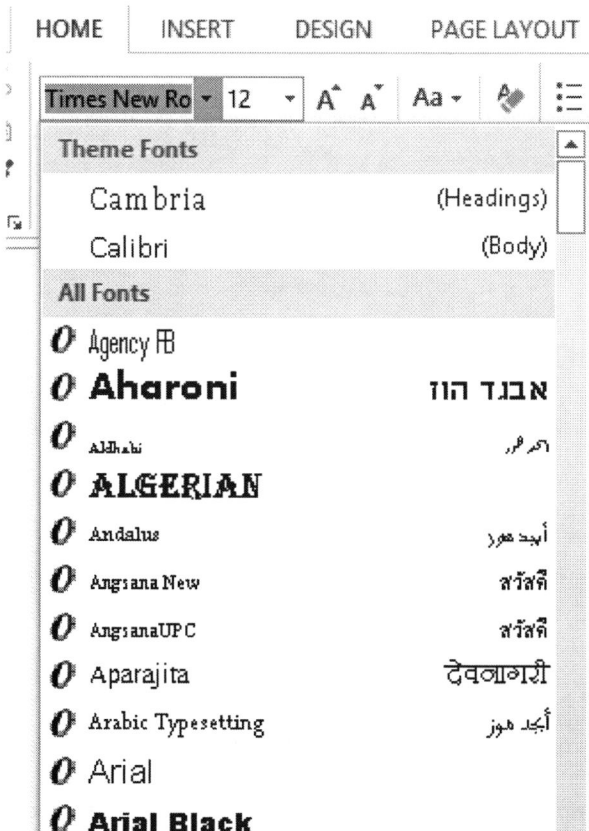

     c) In the **Font** box, type *c* and then scroll in the gallery to **Candara** and select it.

     d) In the **Font Size** box, select the arrow, and choose **12** from the list.

3. Format the text "Our story."

     a) Select the text "Our story."

     b) In the **Font** group, in the **Font Size** box, select the arrow, and choose **16** from the list.

     c) Select the **Italic** button.

     d) On the **Font Color** button, select the arrow, and under **Standard Colors**, select the **Blue** color swatch.

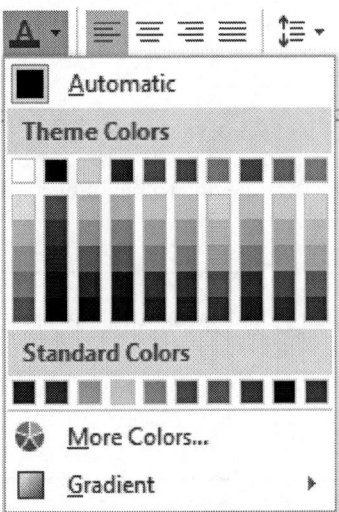

     e) On the **Change Case** button, select the down arrow, and select **Capitalize Each Word**.

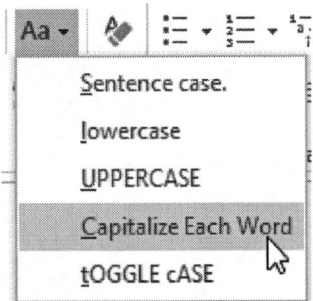

     f) Deselect the text.

4. If necessary, change the font color option back to **Automatic** to reset it back to the default for the document.

     a) Reselect the text "Our story."

     b) On the **Font Color** button, select the arrow, and select **Automatic** from the gallery.

5. Save your changes.

## Text Highlighting Options

In Word, you can draw attention to important information in your document by highlighting it, just as if you had used a highlighting marker. You can turn on highlighting by selecting the **Text Highlight Color** button in the **Font** group. You can then click and drag to highlight the desired text.

The default highlight color is yellow, but you can select the arrow on the **Text Highlight Color** button and then select a different color from the gallery. The button displays the selected color. The highlighter remains active until you select the **Text Highlight Color** button again to turn it off.

## Printing a Document with Highlighted Text

If you are printing your document to a black and white printer, select a light highlight color. This helps ensure that the printed text is readable.

 **Access the Checklist tile on your LogicalCHOICE course screen for reference information and job aids on How to Highlight Text**

# ACTIVITY 3-2
## Highlighting Text

### Data Files

My Bit by Bit Fitness Draft.docx is open.

### Scenario

It might be beneficial to offset the company's contact information from the rest of the document content. There are many ways to do this, but you decide to see what the text will look like with highlighting applied before you try anything else.

---

1. Use Live Preview to view how the first line of text will look with different highlighting colors applied.

   a) At the beginning of the document, select **Visit us at www.bxbfitness.example!**
   b) On the **HOME** tab, in the **Font** group, on the **Text Highlight Color** button, select the arrow to display the color gallery.
   c) Point to various color swatches to view how the text will look with each color applied.

    **Note:** When you enable highlighting from the arrow on the **Text Highlight Color** button, the highlighting button does not remain enabled. If you click directly on the button, it does remain enabled until you select the button again to turn off the highlight.

   d) In the gallery, select the **Yellow** color swatch.

2. Remove the highlight.

   a) Open the **Text Highlight Color** gallery, and select **No Color**.
   b) Drag the highlight marker across the line of highlighted text.
   c) Select the **Text Highlight Color** button to turn off highlighting.

3. Save your changes.

---

## The Format Painter

The *Format Painter* is a handy Word tool that helps you copy the formatting in selected text and apply it to one or more additional selections. You can also use the **Format Painter** to apply basic formatting to graphics, such as fills and borders.

You turn on the **Format Painter** by selecting the text that contains the formatting you want to copy, and then selecting the **Format Painter** button in the **Clipboard** group on the **HOME** tab. You can also activate the **Format Painter** via the **Mini** toolbar.

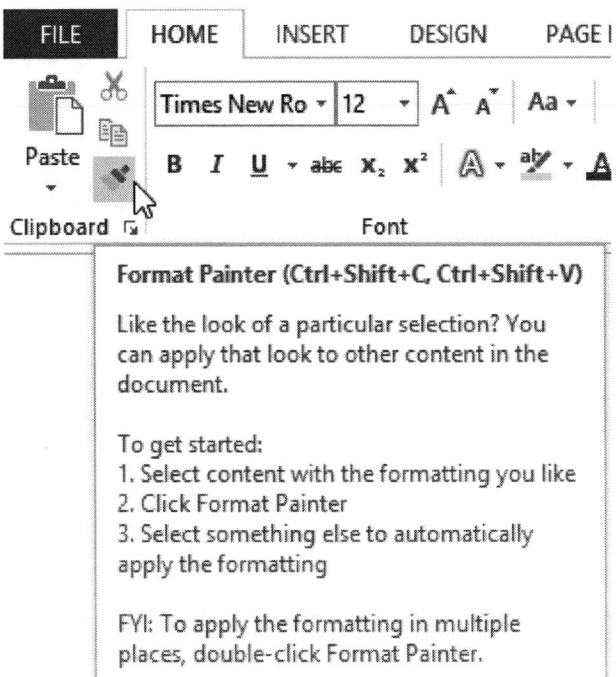

*Figure 3-3: The Format Painter.*

 Access the Checklist tile on your LogicalCHOICE course screen for reference information and job aids on **How to Format Text Using the Format Painter**

# ACTIVITY 3-3
## Using the Format Painter to Format Text

### Before You Begin

My Bit by Bit Fitness Draft.docx is open.

### Scenario

You'd like to create uniformity in the document headings, so you decide to format other headings with the same options that you used for "Our Story." You don't want to take the time to select and reformat every heading with each individual font option, so you decide to use the **Format Painter** to quickly apply those options.

1. Use the **Format Painter** to copy the font options in "Our Story" to the headings "Why Choose Us?" and "What We Offer."

   a) Select "Our Story."

   b) On the **HOME** tab, in the **Clipboard** group, double-click the **Format Painter** button.

    **Note:** You need to double-click the **Format Painter** button in order to apply formatting to more than one selection.

   c) Click and drag over the next two headings to apply the copied formatting.

    **Note:** Depending on your screen size, you might need to use the scroll bar, the mouse wheel, or press the **PgDn** button to see the other headings. Using any of these methods will prevent the **Format Painter** from being deselected.

2. Copy the formatting to the text "The Bit by Bit Golden Rules of Fitness" and "Become a Member Today!"

3. Deselect the **Format Painter**.

4. Save your changes.

# TOPIC B

## Align Text Using Tabs

In addition to applying character formatting options, you'll often want to change the alignment of text to help give it a cleaner appearance. Improperly aligned paragraphs can make a document look sloppy, and cause the reader to miss important information.

### Tabs

Tabs or tab stops help you align text to a specific horizontal location in a document. Using tabs, you can align text to the left, right, or center of the tab stop, or you can set other specialized tab types. You can set one or more tab stops within a paragraph. Pressing **Tab** moves the insertion point, including any text already inserted in the line, to the next tab stop in the document. By default, Word sets a left tab stop every half-inch, within every paragraph.

### Rulers

When aligning text, you can use the rulers that Word provides. Rulers display tab settings and other document layout options, such as page margins. Rulers are displayed at the top of a document and at the extreme left of the document. You can display measurement units as inches, centimeters, millimeters, points, or picas. The default measurement unit is inches.

By default, rulers are hidden. You can display or hide rulers on the **VIEW** tab in the **Show** group.

### Tab Stops on a Ruler

You can use the tab selector on the horizontal ruler to set five types of tabs.

| Tab | Function |
|---|---|
| **Left Tab** ⌊ | Sets the left edge of the text at the tab position and allows the text to flow to the right of the tab stop. |
| **Center Tab** ⊥ | Centers the text around the tab position. |
| **Right Tab** ⌋ | Sets the right edge of the text at the tab position and allows the text to flow to the left of the tab stop. |
| **Decimal Tab** ⊥ | Aligns the decimal point of numbers to the tab position, when numbers are used. |
| **Bar Tab** ▮ | Inserts a vertical line through the paragraph at the tab position. |

### The Tabs Dialog Box

You can easily set and clear tabs by using options in the **Tabs** dialog box, which you can access in the **Paragraph** dialog box by selecting **Tabs**.

| Option | Allows You To |
|---|---|
| **Tab stop position** | Specify the tab location on the ruler. |
| **Default tab stops** | Specify the spacing between default tabs. |

| Option | Allows You To |
|--------|---------------|
| **Alignment** | Change tab alignment. |
| **Leader** | Insert leader characters before a tab, such as dots, dashes, or lines. |
| **Set** | Set the tab position specified in the **Tab stop position** box. |
| **Clear** | Clear the position specified in the **Tab stop position** box. |
| **Clear All** | Clear all tab stops on the ruler. |

 **Access the Checklist tile on your LogicalCHOICE course screen for reference information and job aids on How to Set and Remove Tabs**

# ACTIVITY 3-4
## Setting Tabs

### Before You Begin
My Bit by Bit Fitness Draft.docx is open.

### Scenario
You'd like to give the membership information toward the end of the document a neater appearance, so you decide to align the text using tabs.

1. Display the rulers.
   a) Select **VIEW→Show**.
   b) Check **Ruler**.

2. On the second page of the document, select the membership information, from **Membership** down through **$450**.

   Become a Member Today!

   Membership Level Single Family
   Day Pass$5 n/a
   Monthly $30 $45
   Yearly $300 $450

   Questions?

3. Select a right tab, and set tab stops at the 3", 4", and 5" marks on the ruler.

   a) To the left of the horizontal ruler, click the tab selector until the **Right Tab** icon ⌐ appears.
   b) On the ruler, click at the 3", 4", and 5" marks.

4. Align the text.
   a) Place the insertion point just before **Membership Level** and press **Tab** to align the entire line of text with the first tab stop.
   b) Place the insertion point just before **Single** and press **Tab** to align the word with the second tab stop.
   c) Align **Family** with the third tab stop.
   d) Align the next three lines that contain payment data with the tab stops.

| Membership Level | Single | Family |
|---|---|---|
| Day Pass | $5 | n/a |
| Monthly | $30 | $45 |
| Yearly | $300 | $450 |

5. Save your changes.

# TOPIC C

## Display Text as List Items

Some information is more understandable if it is displayed in sequential order, rather than as a paragraph. You may need to write a set of instructions for performing a certain task. You may want to draw your readers' attention to all the important features of a new company product. This type of information may be misread or overlooked if it is written in paragraph form. The answer? Create a list.

## Lists

A list is a data grouping method in which the items in a group are displayed one after the other. A list often has a lead-in sentence that provides a brief description about the items in it. There can be any number of items in a list. Lists can have a single level or multiple levels and can use various styles of numbers or bullets.

- This is an example of a bulleted list.
- Bulleted lists are unordered.
- Use a bulleted list for items of equal weight.


1. This is an example of a numbered list.
2. Numbered lists are ordered.
3. Use numbered lists for procedures, instructions, etc.

*Figure 3-4: Bulleted and numbered lists.*

## Bulleted Lists

A bulleted list is an unordered list that contains items of equal importance. Items in a bulleted list are grouped under a single heading. Although unordered, bulleted lists can have multiple levels.

You can customize a bulleted list by choosing different bullet styles.

 **Access the Checklist tile on your LogicalCHOICE course screen for reference information and job aids on How to Create a Bulleted List**

# ACTIVITY 3-5
## Creating a Bulleted List

### Before You Begin
My Bit by Bit Fitness Draft.docx is open.

### Scenario
You want to visually emphasize the motivational goals listed in the Why Choose Us? section of the document. You could use a different font style or color, but you don't want the effect to distract from the overall style of the rest of the text. You decide that putting the items in a bulleted list will give them just the right amount of emphasis.

---

1. Create a bulleted list from the motivational questions under "Why Choose Us?"
   a) On the first page, under "Why Choose Us?", select the text for the three questions.

   > Why Choose Us?
   >
   > We believe that regular exercise benefits every body. We believe that it's never too soon—and it's never too late of fitness is, we'll help you make it better.
   >
   > Want to improve your mobility, flexibility, and strength?
   > Want to make new friends, learn Zumba, or join in fitness challenges with others?
   > Do you wish you could play with your kids (or grandkids) more?
   >
   > Whatever your aim, we'll help you get there. Bit by bit.

   b) On the **HOME** tab, in the **Paragraph** group, select the **Bullets** button to add bullets to the questions.

   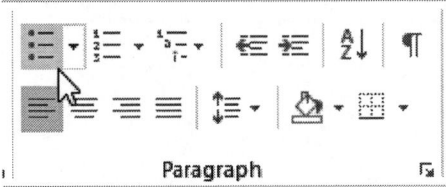

2. Add a new list item.
   a) Click at the end of the third list item and press **Enter**.
      Word automatically adds a bullet.
   b) Type *Are you looking to improve your overall well-being and self-confidence?*
   c) Press **Enter**.

3. Select the **Bullets** button to turn off bulleting.

4. Save your changes.

---

# Numbered Lists

A vertical numbered list contains items that are displayed in a ranked order. Numbered lists can be multilevel, and can be customized using different number or letter styles and formats.

 **Access the Checklist tile on your LogicalCHOICE course screen for reference information and job aids on How to Create a Numbered List**

# ACTIVITY 3-6
## Creating a Numbered List

### Before You Begin
My Bit by Bit Fitness Draft.docx is open.

### Scenario
You know from looking over other company documents that one of the Golden Rules of Fitness is missing. In looking at the rules, you think they would be better presented in a sequential order, so you decide to format the rules as a numbered list, and add the missing rule.

1. Convert the information below the line "The Bit by Bit Golden Rules of Fitness" into a numbered list, and add a new item.

   a) On the second page, find "The Bit by Bit Golden Rules of Fitness" and select all the rules directly below it.

   **The Bit by Bit Golden Rules of Fitness**

   Move more. It doesn't matter what; just move, every day! Garden, walk, jitterbug around the house. Climb more stairs. Swing your arms. Jump on one of our fabulous cardio machines.
   Eat better. Less fast food, more slow food. Cook your own food—it's the only way to know what's in it!
   Lift things. Your toddler. Your dog. The barbells and plates in our free weights area. Strength training helps you build lean muscle and burn more fat.

   b) On the **HOME** tab, in the **Paragraph** group, select the **Numbering** button.

   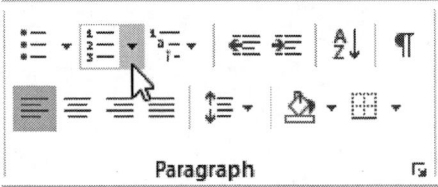

   c) Click at the end of the third item in the list, and press **Enter** to add a new entry.
   d) Type *Exercise with a friend. Find one at Bit by Bit Fitness!* and press **Enter**.
   e) Select the **Numbering** button again to turn off numbering.

2. Save your changes.

# TOPIC D

## Control Paragraph Layout

You can set formatting options that give you a great deal of control over paragraph layout. This can add variety and a professional look to your Word documents. You many not want every paragraph in your documents to look the same. It's possible you'll want to format a certain paragraph with one set of options, and another with a different set of options. Modifying paragraph layout means you can subtly emphasize different portions of your document in a way than enhances the whole.

## Margins

A *margin* is the empty area along the top, bottom, left, and right edges of a page. Margins determine the overall size of a document's text area in relation to the size of the paper it will print on. Additionally, margins dictate the text's vertical or horizontal position on a page. Margins can also affect other layout options, which may be set in relation to the size of the margins.

## Paragraph Alignment Options

*Paragraph alignment* refers to the horizontal position of a paragraph relative to the left and right margins in a document. You can set paragraph alignment options on the **HOME** tab, in the **Paragraph** group, or in the **Paragraph** dialog box.

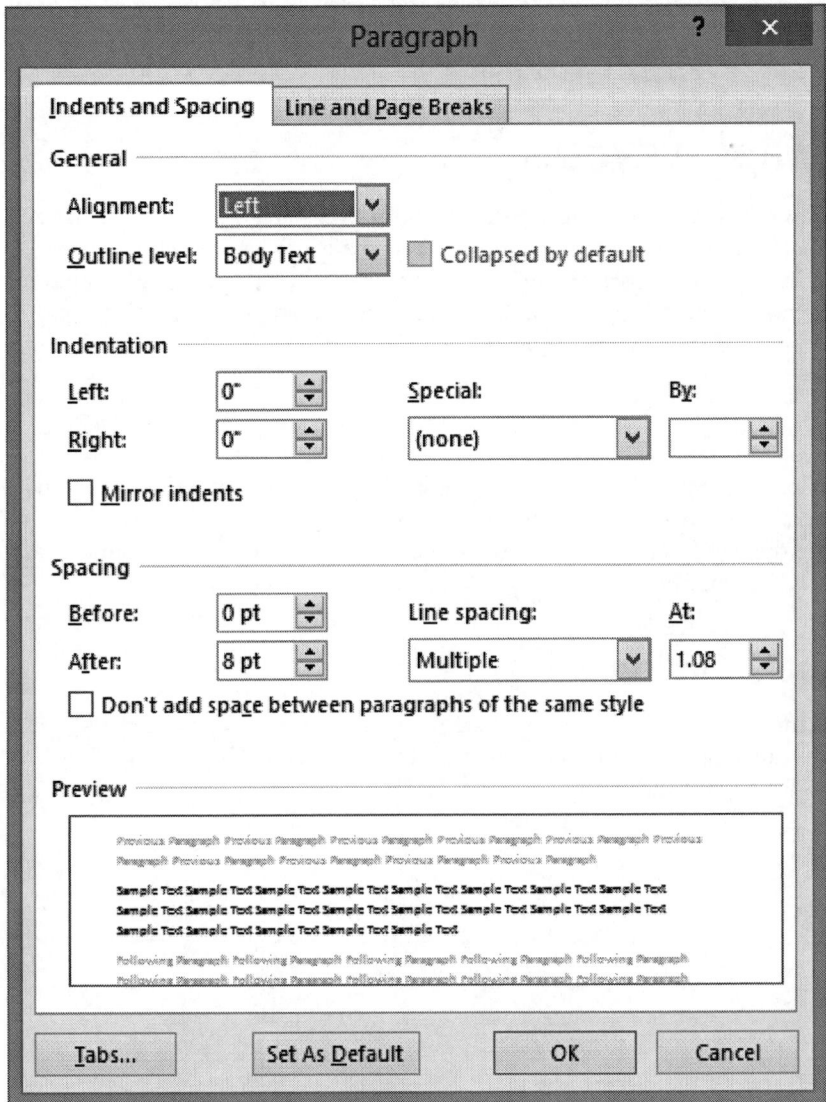

*Figure 3-5: The Paragraph dialog box.*

Paragraph alignment options are described in the following table.

| Option | Description |
|--------|-------------|
| **Align Left** | Aligns the left edge of a paragraph along the left margin. The left edge of the paragraph is even, while the right side is jagged. This is the default alignment option in Word. |
| **Center** | Aligns both sides of a paragraph equidistant from the left and right margins. Both the left and right sides of the paragraph appear jagged. |
| **Align Right** | Aligns the right edge of a paragraph along the right margin. The right side is even, and the left side is jagged. |
| **Justify** | Aligns both sides of a paragraph along the left and right margins. Word adjusts the spacing between the words so that they stretch from the left margin to the right margin. |

 Access the Checklist tile on your **LogicalCHOICE** course screen for reference information and job aids on **How to Set Paragraph Alignment**

# ACTIVITY 3-7
## Setting Paragraph Alignment

### Before You Begin

My Bit by Bit Fitness Draft.docx is open.

### Scenario

All the text in the document, so far, is aligned to the left margin. You think a different position for the paragraph headings might be more visually appealing than the left alignment. You decide to center-align these portions of the document.

---

1.  Center-align the "Our Story" heading.
    a)  Select "Our Story."
    b)  On the **HOME** tab, in the **Paragraph** group, select the **Center** button to center the text.

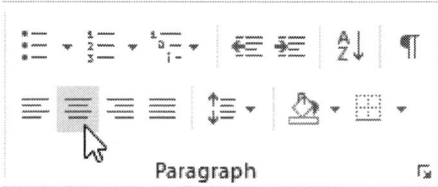

2.  Center-align the "Why Choose Us?," "What We Offer," "The Bit by Bit Golden Rules of Fitness," and "Become a Member Today!" headings.
    a)  Select "Why Choose Us?"
    b)  Press **Ctrl** and select the remaining headings.
    c)  In the **Paragraph** group, select the **Center** button.

3.  Deselect the text.

4.  Save your changes.

---

## Indents

An *indent* refers to the amount of space between a margin and a line or paragraph. You can increase or decrease indents within the page margins. You can also create a negative indent, which pulls the line or paragraph toward the left margin.

## Indent Markers

Indent markers are available on either end of the horizontal ruler. You can set paragraph indentation by selecting the paragraph and dragging the markers to the desired indent position on the ruler.

The various indent markers are described in the following table.

| Marker | Description |
| --- | --- |
| **First Line** | Controls the left boundary of the first line of a paragraph. |

| Marker | Description |
|---|---|
| **Hanging** | Controls the left boundary of every line in a paragraph, except the first line. This is generally used to align the first line with the margin and indent the remainder of the paragraph away from the margin. |
| **Left** | Controls the left boundary of every line in a paragraph. |
| **Right** | Controls the right boundary of every line in a paragraph. |

### Using Indents for Quoted Materials

A standard way to format a lengthy section of a quoted material is to place it within a paragraph that is indented on both sides.

## Indentation Options

You can set precise indentation options in the **Indentation** section of the **Paragraph** dialog box.

| Option | Description |
|---|---|
| **Left** | Sets the left indentation of the paragraph. You can increase or decrease the value in the text box. |
| **Right** | Sets the right indentation of the paragraph. |
| **Special** | Displays whether a **First line** or **Hanging** indent marker is set for the selected paragraph. |
| **By** | Sets the amount of indentation for the special indent in the selected paragraph. |
| **Mirror indents** | Enables you to set the **Inside** and **Outside** indents for a paragraph. When the paragraph is moved from a left page to a right page, or vice versa, the left and right indents are swapped automatically. |

 **Access the Checklist tile on your LogicalCHOICE course screen for reference information and job aids on How to Set Indents in a Paragraph**

# ACTIVITY 3-8
## Setting Indents in a Paragraph

### Before You Begin
My Bit by Bit Fitness Draft.docx is open.

### Scenario
It occurs to you that the information under "What We Offer" is pretty important for potential members. While you could center-align all that text, that won't give the impact you'd like that section to have. You decide instead to apply special indents to the paragraphs to set them apart from the rest of the document.

---

1. Set new indents for the six paragraphs under "What We Offer."
   a) Select the paragraphs under "What We Offer."
   b) On the **HOME** tab, in the **Paragraph** group, click the **Increase Indent** button once to increase the indent by 0.5 inches.

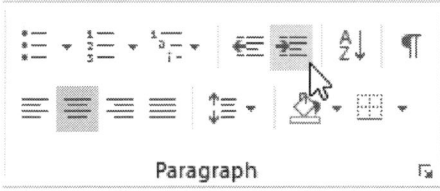

   c) On the horizontal ruler, drag the **Right Indent** marker to the 5" mark.

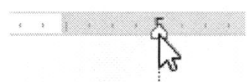

   d) On the horizontal ruler, drag the **Hanging Indent** marker to the 1" mark.

2. Save your changes.

---

## Spacing Options
You can adjust the amount of spacing between lines and paragraphs by using the options in the **Spacing** section of the **Paragraph** dialog box.

| Option | Description |
| --- | --- |
| **Before** | Sets the amount of space before the selected paragraph. The spacing before a paragraph can vary from 0 to 1,584 points. |

| Option | Description |
|---|---|
| After | Sets the amount of space after the selected paragraph. The spacing after a paragraph can vary from 0 to 1,584 points. |
| Line spacing | Sets the amount of space between the lines in a paragraph. You can set it to single space, one and a half space, or double space. You can also set the spacing to an exact or a minimum amount, or choose **Multiple** to adjust the spacing by a percentage of the existing spacing. |
| At | Sets the amount of space between the lines in the selected text. The value entered in this field depends on the **Line spacing** option that is selected. |
| Don't add space between paragraphs of the same style | Does not allow you to add any space between paragraphs that have the same style. |

 **Access the Checklist tile on your LogicalCHOICE course screen for reference information and job aids on How to Set Spacing Options**

# ACTIVITY 3-9
## Setting Spacing Options in a Document

### Before You Begin
My Bit by Bit Fitness Draft.docx is open.

### Scenario
The original author of the Bit by Bit Fitness draft document set the line spacing for all the text at 1, rather than leaving it at the Word 2013 default of 1.15. You think the default line spacing makes for better readability, so you decide to change it back to 1.15. Additionally, you want to add a bit more space between the "Membership" section headings and the membership rates, so that the information there will be more distinct.

---

1. Set the line spacing of the document to 1.15 points.
   a) Select all the text in the document.
   b) On the **HOME** tab, in the **Paragraph** group, select the **Line and Paragraph Spacing** button, and select **1.15** from the list.

2. Increase the line spacing between the heading in the "Membership" section and the membership rate information.
   a) On the third page, place the insertion point just before "Day Pass."
   b) On the **HOME** tab, in the **Paragraph** group, open the **Paragraph** dialog box.
   c) Under **Spacing**, in the **Before** spin box, click the up arrow once to set the spacing at 6 points.
   d) Select **OK** to close the dialog box.

3. Save your changes.

---

# Hyphenation

*Hyphenation* refers to the use of the hyphen, a punctuation mark that joins separate words, or splits words by their syllables. Hyphenation in a paragraph allows you to maintain an even line length and eliminate unwanted gaps in text. You can insert an optional hyphen or a non-breaking hyphen.

Access the hyphenation options on the **PAGE LAYOUT** tab, in the **Page Setup** group.

| Option | Description |
|---|---|
| **None** | Disables hyphenation in the document. This is the default setting in Word. |
| **Automatic** | Instructs Word to automatically hyphenate the document. |
| **Manual** | Allows you to manually hyphenate the words in a document. |

| Option | Description |
|--------|-------------|
| **Hyphenation Options** | Opens the **Hyphenation** dialog box. Here, you can make additional hyphenation adjustments. |

## Non-breaking Spaces and Non-breaking Hyphens

When Word calculates the width of a line and wraps the text to the next line, it breaks the line where there is either a space or a hyphen. In some cases, you may not want to break the line at the place determined by Word. For example, you may want to keep a first name and last name on the same line. Inserting a non-breaking space will accomplish this. Similarly, if you have a hyphenated word that you do not want separated by a line break, insert a non-breaking hyphen.

 **Access the Checklist tile on your LogicalCHOICE course screen for reference information and job aids on How to Set Hyphenation Options**

# ACTIVITY 3-10
## Setting Hyphenation Options

### Before You Begin
My Bit by Bit Fitness Draft.docx is open.

### Scenario
You'd like to use the space in your document more efficiently, so you decide to see whether you can save some space by having Word automatically hyphenate your text.

---

1. Set the hyphenation option to **Automatic**.
   a) On the **PAGE LAYOUT** tab, in the **Page Setup** group, select **Hyphenation**, and choose **Automatic** from the list.
   b) Scroll through the document to observe the hyphenated words. No significant space has been saved, and the text looks choppy.
   c) Return the hyphenation to **None**.

2. Save your changes.

---

# TOPIC E

## Apply Borders and Shading

In addition to applying character formatting options and controlling paragraph layout, you can add borders and shading to portions of text. A list of daily specials on a restaurant menu, for example, will draw the eye if enclosed within a border and filled with color. Applying borders and shading helps to focus a reader's attention right where you want it.

## Borders

A border is a plain or decorative line or pattern that surrounds an object. Borders can be applied to paragraphs, pages, and pictures to draw attention to them. Borders can be applied to the top, bottom, or all four sides of a page or an object.

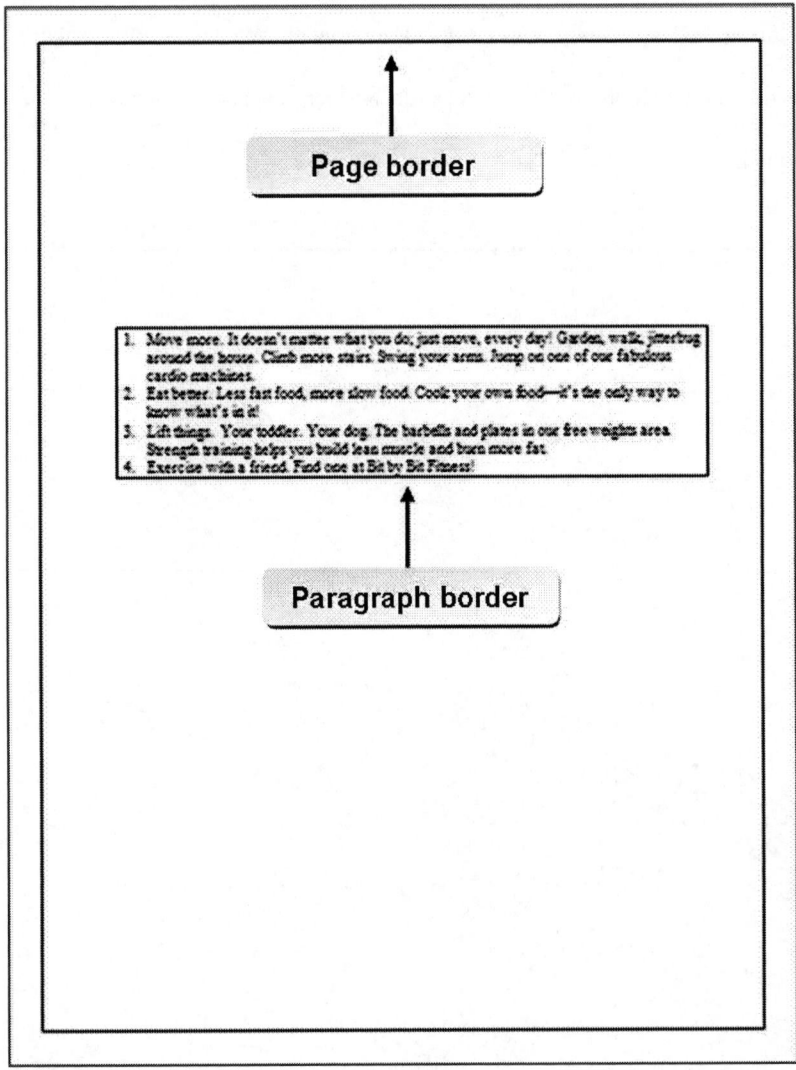

*Figure 3-6: Page and paragraph borders.*

# Types of Borders

On the **HOME** tab, in the **Paragraph** group, you can select from a list of border types by selecting the **Borders** button down arrow. From the list, you can also select **Borders and Shading** to open the **Borders and Shading** dialog box.

Types of borders are described in the following table.

| Border Type | Description |
| --- | --- |
| **Bottom Border** | Inserts a line below the selected object or text. |
| **Top Border** | Inserts a line above the selected object or text. |
| **Left Border** | Inserts a line to the left of the selected object or text. |
| **Right Border** | Inserts a line to the right of the selected object or text. |
| **No Border** | Removes the existing border from the selected object or text. |
| **All Borders** | Applies an outline to the selected table and inserts vertical and horizontal lines between the table cells. This option works only on tables. |
| **Outside Borders** | Applies an outline to the selected object. |
| **Inside Borders** | Inserts vertical and horizontal lines between the table cells. This option works only on tables. |
| **Inside Horizontal Border** | Inserts horizontal lines between the selected rows of a table. This option works only on tables. |
| **Inside Vertical Border** | Inserts vertical lines between the selected columns of a table. This option works only on tables. |
| **Diagonal Down Border** | Inserts a descending diagonal line across a selected cell. This option works only on tables. |
| **Diagonal Up Border** | Inserts an ascending diagonal line across a selected cell. This option works only on tables. |

## Additional Border Options

In addition to selecting a predefined border, there are options in the **Borders** drop-down list that allow users to customize and specify how the borders are displayed in a document.

| Option | Description |
| --- | --- |
| **Horizontal Line** | Inserts a horizontal line on the line where the insertion point is placed. |
| **Draw Table** | Draws a table of the desired size. |
| **View Gridlines** | Shows or hides the gridlines in tables. |
| **Borders and Shading** | Opens the **Borders and Shading** dialog box. |

# Shading

Shading refers to a percentage of color that can be added to the background of objects. Shading can be used to highlight information or to apply a shadow effect. You can apply shading to a line, paragraph, or table data. You can specify a plain fill color, or a pattern in a contrasting color.

On the **HOME** tab, in the **Paragraph** group, you can specify a shading color by selecting the **Shading** button down arrow and choosing a color from the gallery.

1.  Move more. It doesn't matter what you do; just move, every day! Garden, walk, jitterbug around the house. Climb more stairs. Swing your arms. Jump on one of our fabulous cardio machines.
2.  Eat better. Less fast food, more slow food. Cook your own food—it's the only way to know what's in it!
3.  Lift things. Your toddler. Your dog. The barbells and plates in our free weights area. Strength training helps you build lean muscle and burn more fat.
4.  Exercise with a friend. Find one at Bit by Bit Fitness!

*Figure 3-7: Shading applied to bordered text.*

## The Borders and Shading Dialog Box

On the tabs in the **Borders and Shading** dialog box, you can specify precise border and shading options.

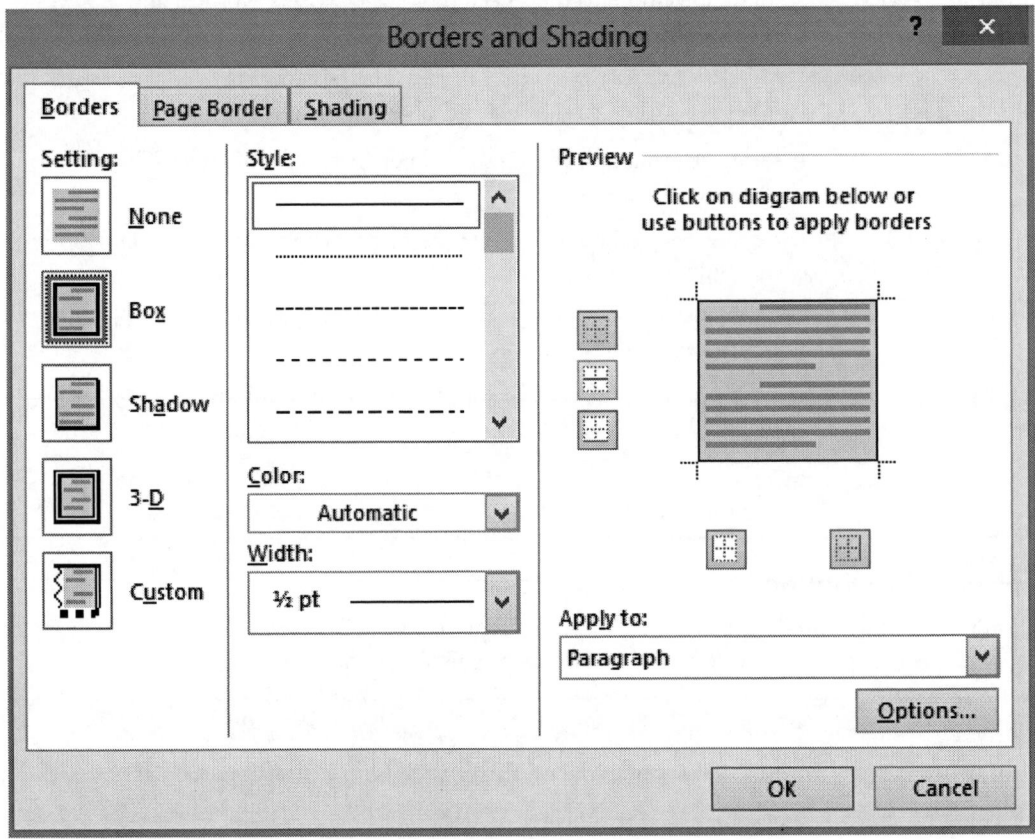

*Figure 3-8: The Borders and Shading dialog box.*

**Borders tab:** Contains options for setting the border type, style, color, width, and the object to which the border will be applied.

**Page Border tab:** Contains options for setting the page border type, style, color, and width. You can also specify predefined art to use as a border, and the pages of the document to which the border will be applied.

**Shading tab**: Contains options for setting the fill color, pattern and pattern color, and the object to which it should be applied.

 **Access the Checklist tile on your LogicalCHOICE course screen for reference information and job aids on How to Add Borders and Shading**

# ACTIVITY 3-11
## Adding Borders and Shading

### Before You Begin
My Bit by Bit Fitness Draft.docx is open.

### Scenario
The document contains a list of the Golden Rules of Fitness. You think it would be helpful to give the list special emphasis by surrounding it with a border and adding a fill color to draw the readers' eyes.

1. Create a box border with a color fill around the numbered list in the section titled "The Bit by Bit Golden Rules of Fitness."
   a) Select the numbered list.
   b) On the **HOME** tab, in the **Paragraph** group, select the arrow on the **Borders** button and select **Borders and Shading** to open the **Borders and Shading** dialog box.
   c) On the **Borders** tab, select **Box**.
   d) In the **Width** box, select the arrow and choose **3/4 pt**.
   e) On the **Shading** tab, in the **Fill** box, select the arrow and choose **Blue, Accent 1, Lighter 80%**.

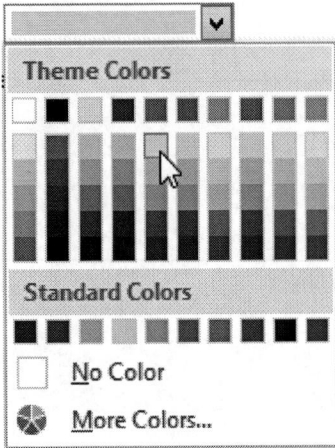

   f) Select **OK** to close the dialog box.
   g) Deselect the text.

2. Save your changes.

# TOPIC F

## Apply Styles

Styles are simply sets of formatting elements that can be applied with a single action. You can use Word's predefined styles, or modify those styles to suit your needs.

## Word Styles

A *Word style* is a collection of appearance settings that can be applied to text with a single click. Using styles is faster than applying formatting options individually, and can ensure consistency of formatting throughout a document. A style may include text formatting options, such as different font typefaces, colors, and effects; and paragraph formatting options, such as line spacing, borders, and shading. You can use built-in styles, modify existing styles, or create custom styles.

This is an example of the normal style.

This is an example of the Heading 1 style.

# This is an example of the Title style.

*This is an example of the Intense Quote style.*

**Figure 3-9: Different styles applied to text.**

## Quick Style Sets

A *Quick Style set* is a package of styles that work well together when applied as a group to text. The styles in the current **Quick Style** set are displayed in the **Styles** group of the **HOME** tab. You can select the **More** button to view the **Quick Styles** gallery. You can quickly change styles by selecting the arrow on the **Change Styles** button and choosing the new styles from the **Style Set** list. You can point to each style set in the list to see a preview of the style in your document.

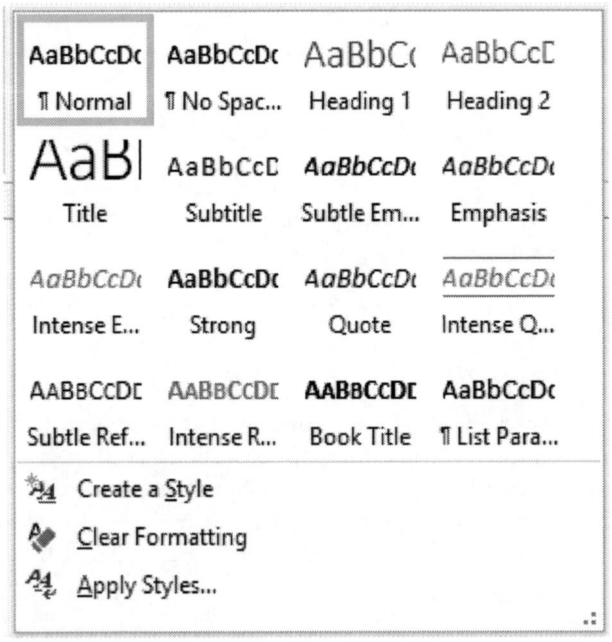

*Figure 3-10: The Quick Styles gallery.*

## The Styles Task Pane

In the **Styles** task pane, you can choose styles and tools that help you work with styles. You can open the **Styles** task pane by selecting the dialog box launcher in the **Styles** group on the **Home** tab.

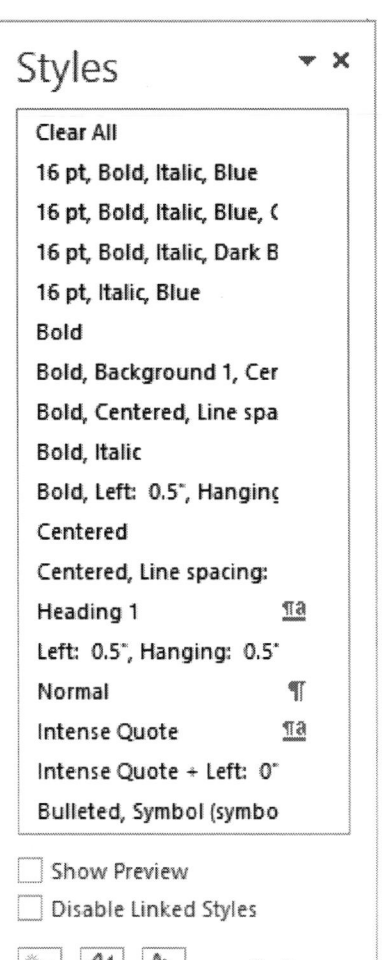

*Figure 3-11: The Styles task pane.*

There are many options available in the **Styles** task pane, as described in the following table.

| Option | Description |
|---|---|
| **Clear All** | Clears all formatting styles that were applied to the selected text. |
| **Show Preview** | Shows a preview of the styles. |
| **Disable Linked Styles** | Disables the styles that can be applied to both paragraphs and individual characters. |
| **New Style** | Opens the **Create New Style from Formatting** dialog box, where you can create a new style and add it to the list. |
| **Style Inspector** | Opens the **Style Inspector** task pane, where you can customize the formatting for a paragraph or text that you have selected. |
| **Manage Styles** | Opens the **Manage Styles** dialog box, which contains tabs with options to edit, recommend, restrict, and set default styles. |
| **Options** | Opens the **Style Pane Options** dialog box, where you can customize the **Styles** task pane. |

### The Apply Styles Task Pane

You can use the **Apply Styles** task pane to modify or reapply a style that is already applied to a document. Open the pane by pressing **Ctrl+Shift+S**. Or, on the **HOME** tab, in the **Styles** group, select the **More** button and choose **Apply Styles**.

### The Style Inspector

The **Style Inspector** is a tool you can use to show the paragraph formatting as separate from the text formatting in your document. This can be useful when you have several types of formatting in a document and find it difficult to determine which formatting is applied to characters, and which to the paragraph.

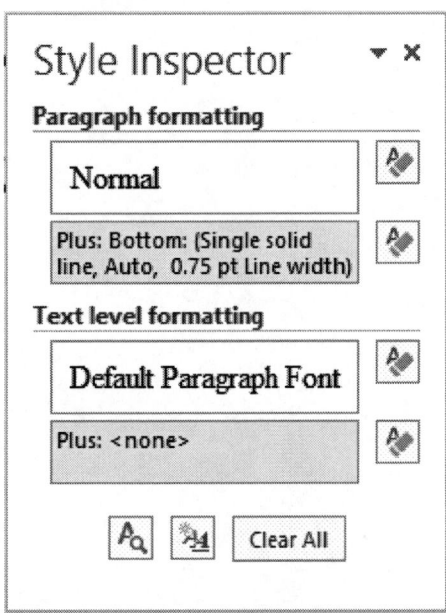

*Figure 3-12: The Style Inspector.*

 Access the Checklist tile on your LogicalCHOICE course screen for reference information and job aids on How to Apply Styles

# ACTIVITY 3-12

## Applying Styles

### Before You Begin

My Bit by Bit Fitness Draft.docx is open.

### Scenario

The text style of the first line in the document seems bland to you, and you'd like to make that information "pop" for the reader, so you decide to apply a more distinctive style. Additionally, you've learned that the first three paragraphs of your document will be copied to another document that uses predefined headings. You decide to format the headings of those paragraphs now, to match the formatting of the document they'll be copied to.

1. Apply the **Intense Quote** style to the first line in the document.
   a) Place the insertion point at the beginning of "Visit us at www.bxbfitness.example!"
   b) On the **HOME** tab, in the **Styles** group, select the **More** button to display the **Styles** gallery.

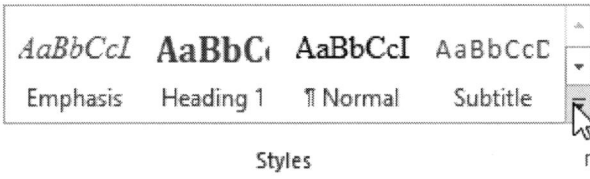

   c) From the gallery, choose **Intense Quote.**

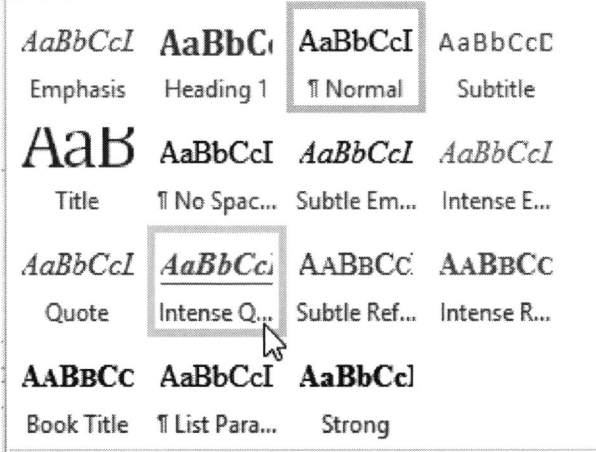

2. Apply the **Heading 1** style to the first three headings in the document.
   a) Place the insertion point at the beginning of the line containing the text "Our Story."
   b) In the **Styles** gallery, select the **Heading 1** style to apply the style to the text.
   c) Apply the **Heading 1** style to "Why Choose Us?" and "What We Offer."

3. Use **Style Inspector** to view the styles in the document.
   a) Select the **Styles** launcher.

b) Select the **Style Inspector** button.

c) Observe the styles in use in the **Style Inspector** pane.
d) Close the **Style Inspector** pane.
e) Close the **Styles** pane.

4. Save your changes.

# TOPIC G

## Manage Formatting

Once you've applied text formatting in a document, you may want to copy, delete, or replace some of it. It can be tedious to search through a long document to find and replace the formatting you want to change. Fortunately, Word gives you tools to easily manage the formatting in your documents.

### The Reveal Formatting Task Pane

You can use the **Reveal Formatting** task pane to help you identify specific formatting elements that are applied to a text selection, including fonts, alignment, indents, document margins, and layouts. You can also compare the formatting of one section to that of another, select text with similar formatting, and apply or clear formatting.

You can open the **Reveal Formatting** task pane by selecting the **Style Inspector** button in the **Styles** task pane, then selecting the **Reveal Formatting** button in the **Style Inspector**. A simpler method is to press **Shift+F1**.

### Clear Formatting Options

There are several methods you can use in Word to clear formatting in a text selection and reset the selection to the default format. These methods include using the **Reveal Formatting** task pane, the **Styles** task pane, the **Style Inspector**, or the **Clear Formatting** button on the **HOME** tab in the **Font** group.

 **Access the Checklist tile on your LogicalCHOICE course screen for reference information and job aids on How to Reveal and Clear Formatting**

## ACTIVITY 3-13
### Revealing and Clearing Formatting

### Before You Begin
My Bit by Bit Fitness Draft.docx is open.

### Scenario
You've decided that some of the italicized words in the document are distracting. In this activity, you'll use the **Reveal Formatting** pane to reveal and clear the unwanted formatting.

---

1. Open the **Reveal Formatting** task pane.
   a) Press **Shift+F1.**

2. Remove the italic style from the items under "What We Offer."
   a) In the document, under the "What We Offer" heading, select the text "Cardiovascular Equipment:."
   b) In the **Reveal Formatting** task pane, observe that both the **Bold** and **Italic** font styles are applied to the text.
   c) In the **Reveal Formatting** task pane, select the arrow in the **Selected text** box, and choose **Select All Text With Similar Formatting**.
   This will select all the bold, italicized formatting.
   d) Select the arrow in the **Selected text** box, and choose **Apply Formatting of Surrounding Text**.

    **Note:** This will remove the italic font style. Choosing this option again would remove the bold style.

   e) Close the **Reveal Formatting** task pane.

3. Save your changes.

---

## Find and Replace Text Formatting Options

You can find all instances of a particular formatting style, or replace one set of format options with another, by using the **Find and Replace** dialog box. When you select the **Format** button on either the **Find** or **Replace** tab, you can specify the format type to search for as well as the format type to replace it with. You can search for and replace character and paragraph formatting, tabs and tab settings, styles, highlighting, and other formatting elements.

 Access the Checklist tile on your **LogicalCHOICE** course screen for reference information and job aids on How to Find and Replace Formatting

# ACTIVITY 3-14
## Finding and Replacing Formatting

### Before You Begin
My Bit by Bit Fitness Draft.docx is open.

### Scenario
You'd like to apply a darker blue to the last two paragraph headings in the document, and also apply a bold font style. There are several ways to accomplish this, but you decide to use the **Find and Replace** dialog box to change the formatting quickly.

---

1. Find the text in the **Blue** color
   a) Position the insertion point at the top of the document.

    **Note:** If you start with the insertion point in the middle of the document, the find and replace works, but you are prompted as to whether you want to search from the beginning of the document. If you have text selected when you begin the find and replace, it searches the selected text first, then the rest of the document, and then prompts you whether you want to search from the beginning of the document.

   b) On the **HOME** tab, in the **Editing** group, select **Replace**.
   c) On the **Replace** tab, clear any text entries in the **Find what** text box.
   d) If necessary, select **More** to expand the list of available options.
   e) Verify that the insertion point is in the **Find what** text box.
   f) Select the **Format** button and select **Font** to open the **Find Font** dialog box.
   g) In the **Font color** gallery, under **Standard Colors**, select **Blue**.

   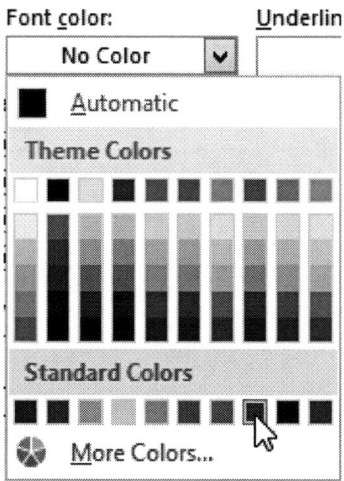

   h) Select **OK** to close the dialog box.

2. Replace the **Blue** text with **Dark Blue, Bold** formatting.
   a) Clear any entries in the **Replace with** text box.
   b) Verify that the insertion point is in the **Replace** text box.
   c) Select **Format**, and then select **Font** to open the **Replace Font** dialog box.

d)  **Note:** Depending on where your insertion point is in the document when you begin the replacement, you might be prompted that no instances were found and asked whether to search from the beginning of the document.

In the **Font color** gallery, select a darker blue color, in the **Font style** list, select **Bold**, and select **OK**.

e) Observe the settings below the **Find** and **Replace** text boxes. This is the formatting that will be found and replaced.

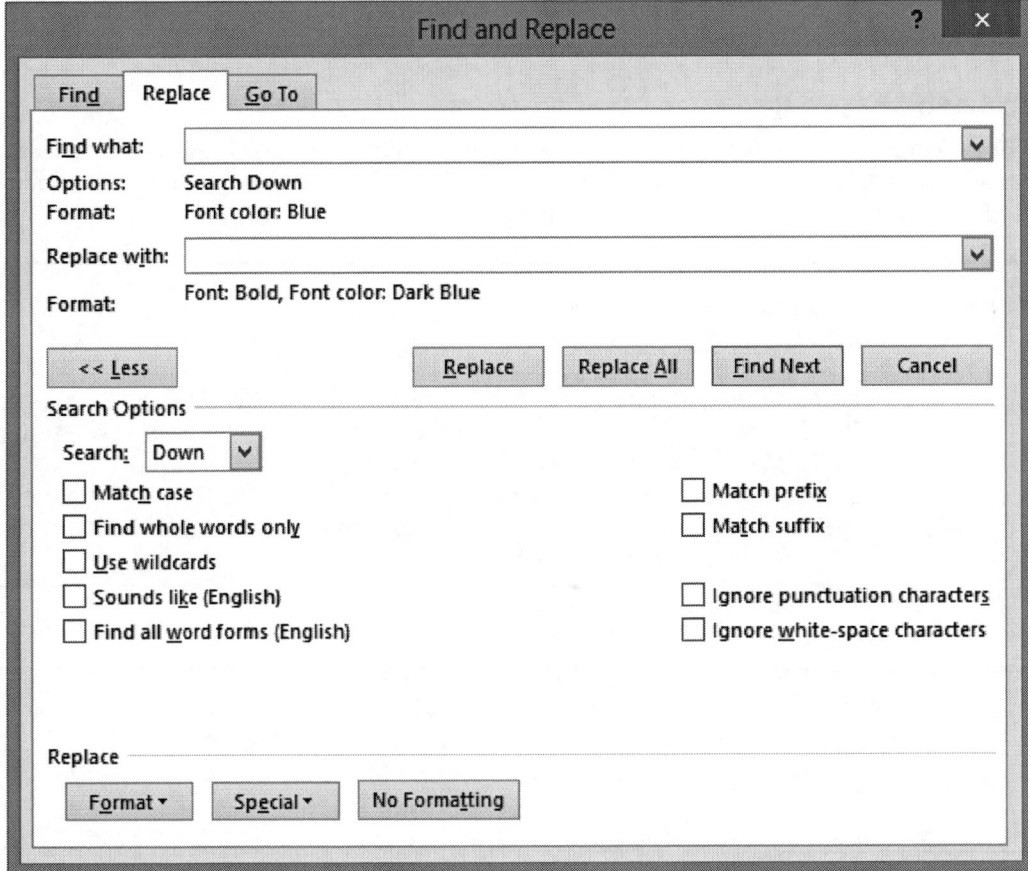

f) Select **Replace All**.
g) Select **OK** in the message box.
h) Close the **Find and Replace** dialog box.

3. Save your changes, and close **My Bit by Bit Fitness Draft.docx**.

# Summary

In this lesson, you applied formatting and paragraph layout options to improve the readability of a Word document. Having so many formatting choices means that you can control the look of individual paragraphs, helping you to bring the appropriate emphasis to different portions of your documents. You also used the **Style Inspector** to view the formatting applied to the document and found and replaced formatted text.

**Which text formatting tools do you think will be the most useful to you when editing your Word documents?**

**Which paragraph formatting tools will you expect to use most often when performing editing tasks?**

 **Note:** Check your LogicalCHOICE Course screen for opportunities to interact with your classmates, peers, and the larger LogicalCHOICE online community about the topics covered in this course or other topics you are interested in. From the Course screen you can also access available resources for a more continuous learning experience.

# 4 Adding Tables

**Lesson Time: 1 hour**

## Lesson Objectives

In this lesson, you will:

- Insert a table into a document.
- Modify the structure of a table.
- Format a table.
- Convert text to a table.

## Lesson Introduction

You've organized information using paragraphs, tabs, and lists. There are times, however, when the best way to present information is in a table. Large quantities of data—for example, long contact lists—can be arranged neatly into rows and columns. Headings can then can be added to clearly identify the data. Using a table to display information can greatly enhance your readers' ability to understand it.

# TOPIC A

## Insert a Table

Let's say you have a list of names and addresses. You could put that information into a numbered or bulleted list, but it might be hard to read each entry. By putting the information into a table, each element of a list item would occupy a single table cell, and each list item would occupy a single row. This helps to make the data as a whole easier to comprehend.

### Tables

A *table* is a container that is used to organize text, numerical data, or graphics. Tables consist of individual cells that are arranged in vertical columns and horizontal rows. Each cell stores a piece of information. A table can have specialized table formats, such as borders drawn around some or all of the cells, or shading in rows or columns.

| | Monday | Tuesday | Wednesday | Thursday | Friday | Saturday | Sunday |
|---|---|---|---|---|---|---|---|
| 9:15-10:00 | Gentle Yoga | | Gentle Yoga | | Yoga | Intro to Movement | |
| 10:00 | Deep Stretch | | | Deep Stretch | | Beg. Hula Hoop | |
| 11:00 | | Gentle Yoga | | | | | |
| 12:00 | Beg. Pilates | | Pilates | | Pilates | | |
| 4:30 | Zumba! | | Zumba! | | Zumba! | | |
| 6:00 | Group Strength | Kickboxing | Group Strength | Kickboxing | Tai Chi | | |
| 7:15 | Step Fit | Classic Rock Aerobics | Step Fit | Classic Rock Aerobics | Ballroom Dance I | Ballroom Dance II | |
| 8:15 | | | | | Dance Practice | Dance and Social Hour | |

*Figure 4–1: A table containing data organized into rows and columns.*

### Using Tables to Control Page Layout

Tables can organize both text and graphics and can help simplify your page layout. Using tables, you can arrange content in columns, apply different backgrounds and colors for different areas of a page, and adjust the size and width of different text areas. You can even insert a table into another table, and remove borders to hide the table structure. This flexibility with tables helps you easily manage even a complex page layout.

### Table Creation Options

Microsoft® Word 2013 provides several options for creating tables. You can access these options on the **INSERT** tab, in the **Tables** group, from the **Table** drop-down list.

The following table describes the various methods for creating a table.

| Option | Description |
|---|---|
| **Insert Table** | Allows you to draw over a grid to select the number of rows and columns. |

| Option | Description |
|---|---|
| **Insert Table** | Opens the **Insert Table** dialog box. Here, you can specify values for the number of rows and columns. You can also specify how data should fit into the cells. |
| **Draw Table** | Allows you to draw a more complex table. |
| **Convert Text to Table** | Allows you to convert text that contains a separator between the information for each table cell into a table. Separators are often tabs, commas, hyphens, or paragraphs. |
| **Excel Spreadsheet** | Allows you to insert a Microsoft® Excel® spreadsheet as a table. When you select the inserted table, Word provides you with all the features and tools available in Excel as options on the ribbon. |
| **Quick Tables** | Allows you to select from a gallery of predefined table styles. |

## Contextual Tabs

*Contextual tabs* are additional tabs that appear on the ribbon when you work with objects such as tables, pictures, or shapes. The commands and options available on these tabs are restricted to those that manipulate the objects associated with the tab. You can switch between the contextual tabs and the core tabs as needed.

## Table Navigation Methods

You can navigate in a table efficiently by using keyboard techniques.

| Key/Keys | Function |
|---|---|
| **Tab** or **Right Arrow** | Moves the insertion point one cell to the right. |
| **Shift+Tab** or **Left Arrow** | Moves the insertion point one cell to the left. |
| **Down Arrow** | Moves the insertion point down one row. |
| **Up Arrow** | Moves the insertion point up one row. |

### Nonprinting Characters in Tables

There are several nonprinting characters that are specific to tables in Word. Each cell contains an end-of-cell marker to indicate the end of that cell. To the right of each row is an end-of-row marker that indicates the end of that row. Column markers are displayed in the ruler, and can be dragged to resize columns. In addition to these markers, Word can also display nonprinting gridlines around the table cells. Gridlines are sometimes called boundaries. If a table has borders applied to it, the gridlines will be displayed beneath the borders.

## Quick Tables

*Quick Tables* are preformatted tables that contain sample data. You can use the **Quick Tables** gallery to quickly insert a new table with a predefined style. You can then replace the placeholder text in the table with your own data. In Word, you can access the **Quick Tables** gallery can from the **Tables** group on the **INSERT** tab. There are different types of **Quick Tables**, such as calendars, double tables, and tables with subheadings. **Quick Tables** may apply a coordinated set of different fonts and column delimiters to a table.

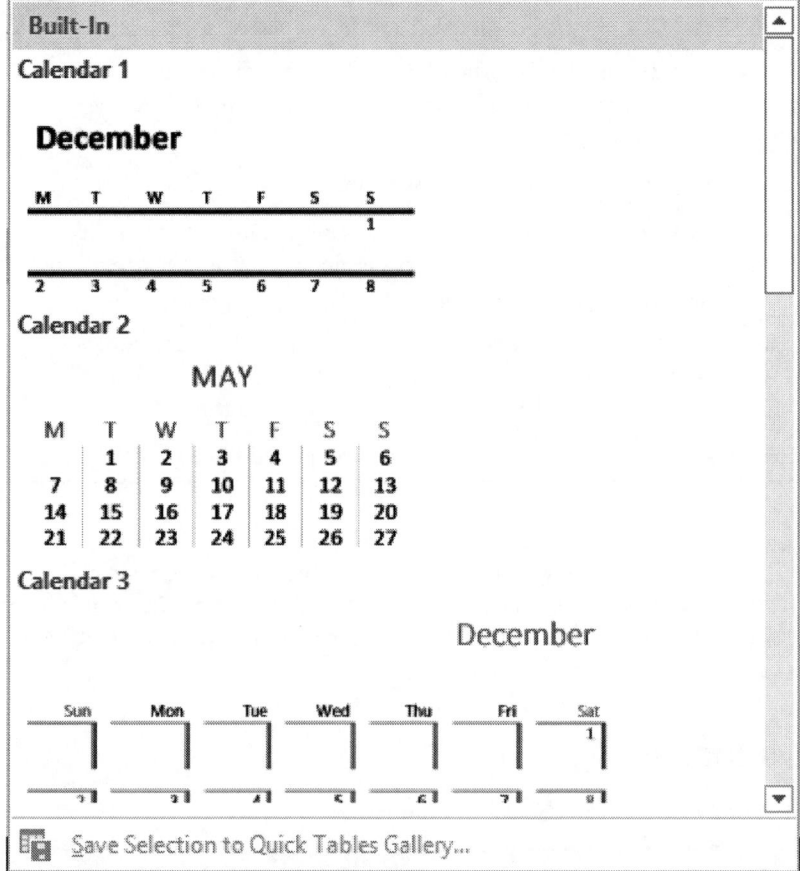

*Figure 4-2: The Quick Tables gallery.*

 Access the Checklist tile on your LogicalCHOICE course screen for reference information and job aids on How to Insert a Table

# ACTIVITY 4-1

## Inserting a Table in a Document

### Data Files

C:\091024Data\Adding Tables\Schedules.docx

### Scenario

A coworker began work on a document that contains various schedules for the Bit by Bit Fitness center, but was given another assignment before he could finish his work. He has asked you to create a table in the document that will hold the schedule for the Community Room. In this activity, you'll insert a table to use as the schedule, and enter headings into it.

---

1. Navigate to the **C:\091024Data\Adding Tables** folder, open **Schedules.docx,** and save it as *My Schedules.docx*

2. Using the **Insert Table** dialog box, insert a table in the document under **Community Room Schedule**. The table should have six columns and four rows.

   a) Click in the blank line under **Community Room Schedule**.
   b) On the **INSERT** tab, in the **Tables** group, select **Table**, and select **Insert Table** from the list.
   c) In the **Insert Table** dialog box, in the **Number of columns** spin box, enter **6,** and in the **Number of rows** spin box, enter *4*

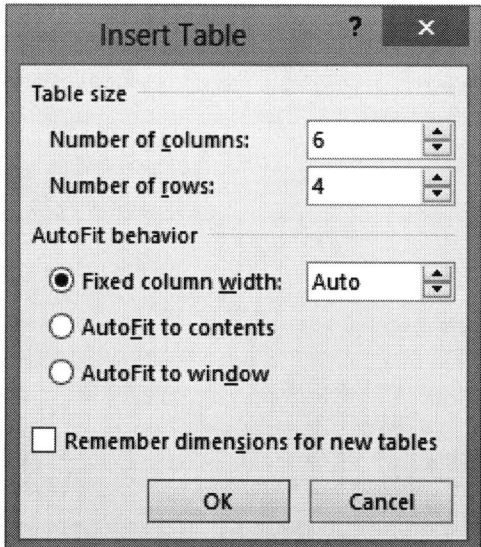

   d) Select **OK** to create the table.

3. Enter text into the first row of the table.

   a) Press **Tab** to move the cursor to the second cell in the first row.
   b) Type *Monday* and press **Tab**.
   c) In the cell, type *Tuesday*
   d) In the remaining cells of the first row, add *Wednesday*, *Thursday*, and *Friday*

4. Enter text into the first column of the table.

a)  In the second cell of the first column, type *10:00* and press the **Down Arrow** key.

b)  In the third cell of the first column, type *12:00* and press the **Down Arrow** key.

c)  In the final cell in the column, type *5:00*

|       | Monday | Tuesday | Wednesday | Thursday | Friday |
|-------|--------|---------|-----------|----------|--------|
| 10:00 |        |         |           |          |        |
| 12:00 |        |         |           |          |        |
| 5:00  |        |         |           |          |        |

5.  Save your changes.

# TOPIC B

## Modify a Table

As you work with tables, you may find that you want to make changes to the table structure. You may have new data to add, making it necessary to add rows and/or columns. You might find that merging some data in the table is a better way to present it, or that the data is more comprehensible if cells are resized. Word provides several methods for adjusting the structure of your table so you can keep your data neat and well organized.

## Table Selection Methods

Before you can make certain changes to the table structure, you'll need to select the table itself, or its elements.

| To Select | Do This |
| --- | --- |
| A row or rows | Move the mouse pointer to the blank space at the left of the desired row. When the mouse pointer changes to a right-tilted white arrow, click to select the row. You can also select several rows by clicking and dragging the mouse pointer along the required number of rows. |
| A column or columns | Move the mouse pointer to the top or bottom border of the column until the mouse pointer changes to a black down arrow, and then click to select the column. You can also select several columns by clicking and dragging the mouse pointer along the required number of columns. |
| A cell or cells | Move the mouse pointer to the blank space before the text in a cell. When the mouse pointer changes to a right-tilted dark arrow, click to select the cell. To select a group of cells, drag over the cells, or click a cell, hold down **Shift**, and click the last cell. |
| The entire table | Point to the table until the table selection box appears outside the top-left corner of the table, and then click the box. Or, on the **LAYOUT** tab, in the **Table** group, from the **Select** drop-down list, choose **Select Table**. |

## The TABLE TOOLS LAYOUT Contextual Tab

The **TABLE TOOLS LAYOUT** contextual tab contains groups with options to modify the structure of a table. Options available in the various groups are described in the following table.

| Group | Options |
| --- | --- |
| **Table** | Select elements of the table, and view table gridlines and table properties. |
| **Rows & Columns** | Insert or delete rows and columns, and other table elements. |
| **Merge** | Merge and split cells, and split the table. |
| **Cell Size** | Change the height of rows and width of columns; make multiple rows or columns the same size. |
| **Alignment** | Modify the alignment of the text in a table and change the direction in which the text is entered. You can also change the default value of each cell's margins. |

| Group | Options |
|-------|---------|
| Data | Sort, calculate, or convert the information in a table to text. You can also use this group to repeat the header rows on every page when a table extends beyond a single page. |

*Figure 4–3: The TABLE TOOLS LAYOUT contextual tab.*

## The Table Properties Dialog Box

Tabs in the **Table Properties** dialog box allow you to specify options for rows and columns, individual cells, or an entire table. You can open this dialog box from the **TABLE TOOLS LAYOUT** contextual tab, in the **Table** group, by selecting **Properties**. Each tab in the dialog box contains several options.

| Tab | Options |
|-----|---------|
| **Table** | Set the size, alignment, and text wrapping of a table. |
| **Row** | Set the height of the selected row. This tab also allows you to apply a page break and navigate to the previous or next row. |
| **Column** | Modify the size of the selected column. This tab also allows you to navigate to the previous or next column. |
| **Cell** | Modify the size and vertical alignment of text in the selected cell. |
| **Alt Text** | Enter alternative text information, such as a title for the table. This information is shown when a table is displayed in a web browser. |

> **Access the Checklist tile on your LogicalCHOICE course screen for reference information and job aids on How to Insert and Delete Cells, Rows, and Columns**

# ACTIVITY 4–2
## Inserting and Deleting Rows and Columns

### Before You Begin
My Schedules.docx is open.

### Scenario
You've created a basic table for the Community Room Schedule. You realize that you've forgotten to add columns for Saturday and Sunday, and that the Community Room will also have scheduled events planned for later in the evening on some days.

1. Add a **Saturday** column to the end of the table.
   a) Click in any cell in the last column of the table.
   b) On the **TABLE TOOLS LAYOUT** contextual tab, in the **Rows & Columns** group, select **Insert Right** to insert a new column to the right of the last column.
   c) In the column heading, type *Saturday*

2. Add a **Sunday** column to the end of the table.

3. Use **Tab** to add a new row to the bottom of the table.
   a) Click in the last cell of the last row.
   b) Press **Tab**.
   c) In the first cell of the new row, type *6:00*

4. Use the **TABLE TOOLS LAYOUT** contextual tab to add a new row to the bottom of the table.
   a) On the **TABLE TOOLS LAYOUT** contextual tab, in the **Rows & Columns** group, select **Insert Below** to add another row.
   b) In the first cell of the new row, type *7:00*

5. Delete the fourth row of the table.
   a) Point your cursor to the left of the **5:00** row until the pointer changes to a small black arrow, and then double-click to select the entire row.
   b) In the **Rows & Columns** group, select **Delete**, and then select **Delete Rows**.

|       | Monday | Tuesday | Wednesday | Thursday | Friday | Saturday | Sunday |
|-------|--------|---------|-----------|----------|--------|----------|--------|
| 10:00 |        |         |           |          |        |          |        |
| 12:00 |        |         |           |          |        |          |        |
| 6:00  |        |         |           |          |        |          |        |
| 7:00  |        |         |           |          |        |          |        |

6. Save your changes.

 **Access the Checklist tile on your LogicalCHOICE course screen for reference information and job aids on How to Manipulate Table Rows and Columns**

# ACTIVITY 4-3
## Moving and Resizing Columns

### Before You Begin
My Schedules.docx is open.

### Scenario
You'd like to modify the table structure to make Sunday the first day of the schedule week. You've also noticed that the table you've created is a little narrower than the table above it, so you decide to resize the last column border in your table to line up with the last column border of the table above.

1. In the Community Room Schedule, move the **Sunday** column to the beginning of the table.
   a) Point to the top of the **Sunday** column until the pointer becomes a small, black arrow, and click to select the column.
   b) Cut the selection.
   c) Place the insertion point in the first cell of the **Monday** column.
   d) Paste the cut selection.

2. In the Community Room Schedule table, resize the right border of the **Saturday** column so that it lines up with the right border of the Fitness Studio Schedule table **Saturday** column.
   a) Position the mouse pointer at the right boundary of the **Saturday** column until it changes to a double-headed arrow.
   b) Drag the gridline to line up with the right boundary of the Fitness Studio Schedule table **Saturday** column.

| Dance Practice | Dance and Social Hour | |
|---|---|---|
| | | |
| lay | Saturday | |
| | | |

3. Save your changes.

# TOPIC C

# Format a Table

Once you've added a table to your document, you'll probably want to make adjustments to its appearance. You'll not only want to draw attention to the table data, but you'll want the table formatting to complement other formatting elements in the document.

## Table Styles

You can easily format a table by applying a table style. A table style contains a set of table-specific formatting instructions. Table styles include borders, shading, colors, cell alignment, table fonts, and separate formats for the first column or row. There are various table styles to choose from. You can also modify an existing style or build a new style and add it to the gallery.

## The TABLE TOOLS DESIGN Contextual Tab

The **TABLE TOOLS DESIGN** contextual tab contains several design options to help you easily format your table. Each group on the tab contains styling tools and commands.

| Group | Options |
|---|---|
| **Table Style Options** | Modify a table style by formatting specified rows or columns. |
| **Table Styles** | Format a table by using a set of predefined styles. Includes options to apply a background color and borders. |
| **Draw Borders** | Draw borders on a table. Includes options to change the line style, color, and thickness of the border. You can also erase the border. |

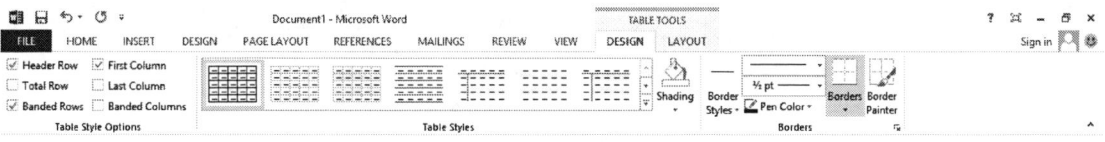

*Figure 4-4: The TABLE TOOLS DESIGN contextual tab.*

 **Access the Checklist tile on your LogicalCHOICE course screen for reference information and job aids on How to Format a Table**

# ACTIVITY 4-4
## Formatting a Table

### Before You Begin
My Schedules.docx is open.

### Scenario
The table you've created is very plain, which makes it difficult to distinguish one piece of information from another. You'd like to make it look more appealing, as well as help emphasize the content within it. You decide to apply some formatting options to enhance the table's appearance.

1. Apply the **Grid Table 5 Dark - Accent 1** table style to the Community Room Schedule.
   a) Verify that the insertion point is somewhere within the table.
      The **TABLE TOOLS DESIGN** contextual tab is only active when the insertion point is within the boundaries of a table.
   b) On the **TABLE TOOLS DESIGN** contextual tab, in the **Table Styles** group, select the **More** button to display the **Table Styles** gallery.
   c) If necessary, scroll down and select the style **Grid Table 5 Dark - Accent 1** style.

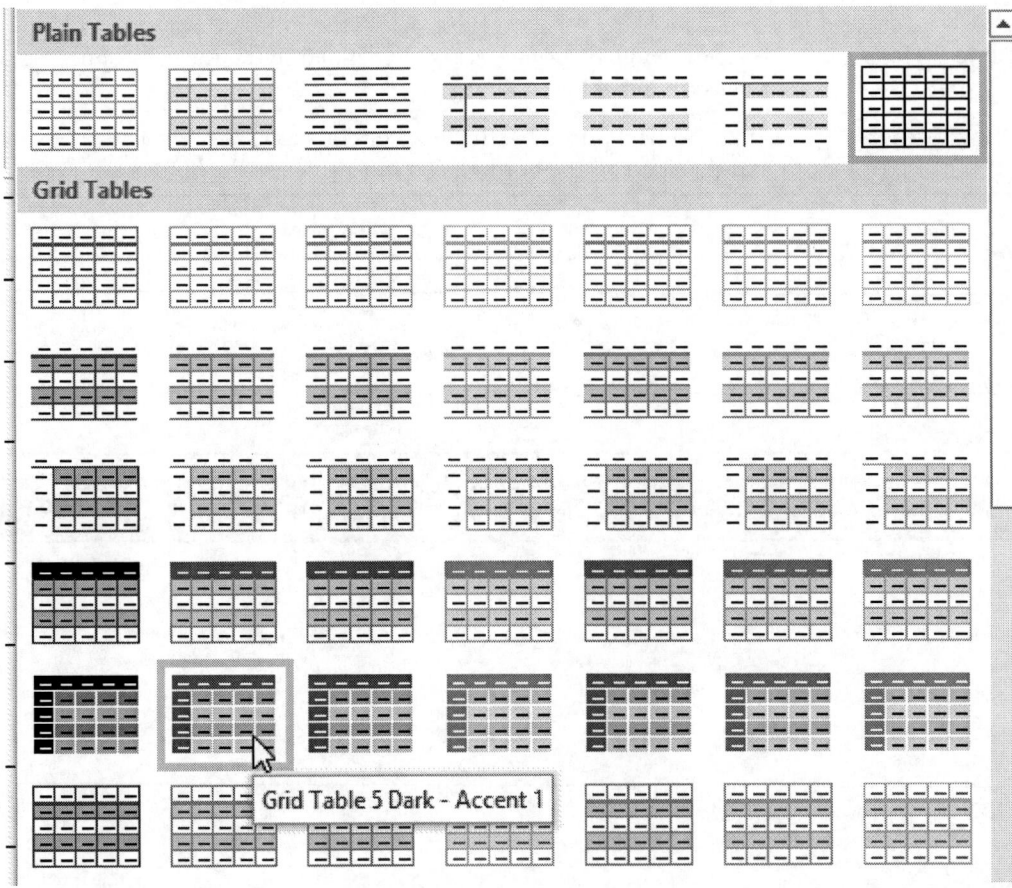

2. Turn off banded rows in the table, and turn on banded columns.

    a) In the **Table Style Options** group, uncheck **Banded Rows**.

    b) Check **Banded Columns**.

3. Apply left and right borders to the table, using a line width of 2 1/4 points.

    a) In the **Borders** group, select the arrow on the **Borders** button and choose **Borders and Shading** to open the **Borders and Shading** dialog box.

    b) Under **Color** select **Blue**.

    c) Under **Style,** verify that the solid, single-line style is selected.

    d) Under **Width**, select **2 1/4 pt** from the drop-down list.

    e) In the **Preview** pane, select the left and right borders of the diagram.

    f) Select **OK** to close the dialog box and apply the borders.

4. Apply inside borders with a line width of 1/4 pt to the banded cells within the table.

    a) Select the banded cells. Do not include the row or column headings.

    b) In the **Borders** group, from the **Line Weight** drop-down list, select **1/4 pt**.

    c) From the **Pen Color** drop-down list, select **Blue**.

    d) Select the arrow on the **Borders** button and select **Inside Borders** from the list.

5. Save your changes.

# TOPIC D

## Convert Text to a Table

In addition to creating blank tables in which you manually enter your data, you can also take existing text and convert it to table form. Similarly, you can convert content in a table to text. These are useful options when you think your existing information could be better presented as text or as a table, but don't want to have to manually re-enter it in the new format.

### The Convert Text to Table Dialog Box

If you've used tabs to create columns of data in a document, you can convert the tabbed text to a table by using the options in the sections of the **Convert Text to Table** dialog box. Text that is separated by paragraphs or commas can also be converted to table form. Each section of the dialog box contains options to create the table.

| Section | Description |
|---|---|
| **Table size** | Provides options to specify the number of rows and columns to suit the table content. |
| **AutoFit behavior** | Provides options to specify how the table columns are sized to fit the contents in the table. Columns can be of fixed width, equally sized to fit the document width, or variably sized depending on the content of each column. |
| **Separate text at** | Provides options to specify whether paragraphs, tabs, commas, or any other option should be considered as a delimiter to split the text into table cells when converting the text to a table. |

### The Convert Table To Text Dialog Box

You can use the **Convert Table To Text** dialog box to convert the text in a table to paragraph format. It provides options to separate the data in the table by using paragraph marks, tabs, commas, or other delimiting characters, when it is converted to text. You can access the **Convert Table To Text** dialog box from the **Data** group on the **TABLE TOOLS LAYOUT** contextual tab.

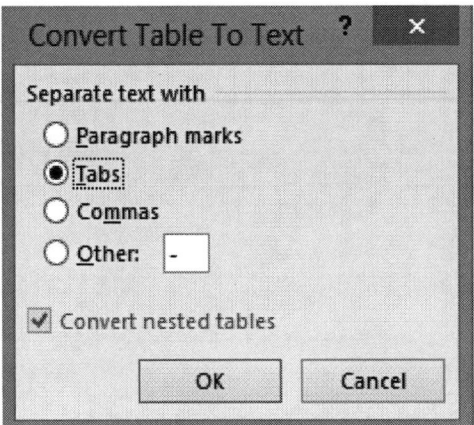

*Figure 4–5: The Convert Table To Text dialog box.*

**Access the Checklist tile on your LogicalCHOICE course screen for reference information and job aids on How to Convert Text to a Table**

# ACTIVITY 4–5
## Converting Data

### Before You Begin
My Schedules.docx is open.

### Scenario
You've noticed that the walk-in personal training schedule is tabbed data. You decide that the information would look better if it were put into table form. On the other hand, you think the trainer hours information, since there is so little of it, would be more readable if it were in tabbed text form. You may choose to apply other style options at a later time, but for now, you just want to convert data to a proper format.

---

1. Convert the walk-in personal training data into a table that separates the data using tabs, and which fits the data exactly.

   a) On the second page of the document, under "Walk-in personal training," place the insertion point just before "Day" and drag to select all the schedule data through the last instance of "Mary Prioletti".

   b) On the **INSERT** tab, in the **Tables** group, select the **Table** button arrow and choose **Convert Text to Table** to open the **Convert Text to Table** dialog box.

   c) In the dialog box, verify that the value in the **Number of columns** spin box is **3**.

   d) Under **AutoFit behavior**, select **AutoFit to contents**.

   e) Under **Separate text at**, verify that **Tabs** is selected.

   f) Select **OK** in the **Convert Text to Table** dialog box.

2. Convert the Trainer/hrs table to text.

   a) Click in any cell of the Trainer/hrs table.

   b) On the **TABLE TOOLS LAYOUT** contextual tab, in the **Data** group, select **Convert to Text** to open the **Convert Table To Text** dialog box.

   c) In the dialog box, verify that **Tabs** is selected, and then select **OK**.

3. Save your changes, and close the file.

---

# Summary

In this lesson, you organized data into tables. Arranging data into table form, rather than into a list or a paragraph, can help make the information easier for the reader to understand and absorb. Applying table styles will help you format your tables with one click, and you can modify any style to create an eye-catching way to highlight your data.

**In what way will using tables in Word help you create better documents?**

**What sort of information might you want to present in table form?**

 **Note:** Check your LogicalCHOICE Course screen for opportunities to interact with your classmates, peers, and the larger LogicalCHOICE online community about the topics covered in this course or other topics you are interested in. From the Course screen you can also access available resources for a more continuous learning experience.

# 5 | Managing Lists

**Lesson Time: 30 minutes**

## Lesson Objectives

In this lesson, you will:

- Sort a list.
- Renumber a list.
- Customize a list.

## Lesson Introduction

You've created lists in order to improve the readability of certain types of information. Sometimes, lists need to be edited. Either you need to add items, delete them, or modify them in some way. And, not all lists fit into a simple, one-level bulleted or numbered format. The more types of lists you use, the more you'll need options to perform such tasks as creating categories within a list, showing relationships between list items, and customizing a list's appearance for an effective visual impact. Microsoft® Word 2013 provides you with many useful features that help you do all of this and more when working with lists.

# TOPIC A

## Sort a List

When you create a list for the first time, the list items appear in the order you enter them. You may find that you need to reorder the items, perhaps alphabetically or by some other criteria. Instead of re-creating the entire list, or cutting and pasting items to put them where you want them, you can choose to sort the list. Sorting a list helps you to rearrange it in a logical order, and this means that you don't have to worry about the sequence of the items when you enter them. Also, you can display the information in your list in different ways, depending on your needs at any given moment.

### Sort Types

You can sort lists by three types of data, in ascending or descending order.

| Sort Type | Sort Rule |
|-----------|-----------|
| **Text** | Organizes list items that begin with punctuation marks first, then by items beginning with numbers, and then by individual digits (for instance, 36 will sort before 4). Finally, items beginning with letters are sorted alphabetically. **Ascending** sorts text from A to Z, while **Descending** sorts text from Z to A. |
| **Number** | Arranges list items by numbers present anywhere in the item. It sorts by numeric value (for instance, 4 will sort before 36). **Ascending** sorts numbers from the lowest to the highest; **Descending** sorts from highest to lowest. |
| **Date** | Sorts list items by both time and date in chronological order. **Ascending** sorts from earliest to most recent; **Descending** sorts from most recent to earliest. |

### Sort Fields

A *sort field* is a list item that can be used as the criterion for sorting a list. Sort fields enable you to perform multiple-level sorts on a list. Let's say you want to sort a contact list by state, and then by city. The state would occupy one sort field, and the city would occupy another. Multiple sort fields in a list item are separated by a standard character called the *sort field separator*. In Word, tabs, commas, or any character you specify can be used as the sort field separator.

If you select headings at the top of the list, the sort fields are identified in the **Sort Text** dialog box by the headings. If the list doesn't have headings or if you don't select them for the sort, then the sort fields are identified as **Field 1**, **Field 2**, and so on.

 Access the Checklist tile on your **LogicalCHOICE** course screen for reference information and job aids on **How to Sort a List**

# ACTIVITY 5–1

## Sorting a List

### Data Files

C:\091024Data\Managing Lists\Report Draft.docx

### Scenario

You've been assigned to help shape a document containing information that will be used to create a report on membership retention, which will be sent to other Bit by Bit Fitness centers. As you look at the first part of the document, which is a list of locations of the other fitness centers, the information seems poorly organized, and almost random. You decide that the list could be presented in a more logical order, which will help you prepare the distribution of the report later.

---

1. Navigate to the **C:\091024Data\Managing Lists** folder, open **Report Draft.docx**, and save it as *My Report Draft.docx*

2. On the first page, sort the "Locations" list, in ascending order, first by state, then by city, and then by zip code.

    a) Select all the entries including the list column headings.

    >  **Caution:** Be sure not to select the empty rows below the list as they would be included in the sort if they were selected.

    b) On the **HOME** tab, in the **Paragraph** group, select the **Sort** button to open the **Sort Text** dialog box.

    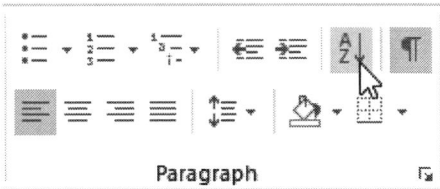

    c) Under **My list has** select **Header row**.
    d) In the dialog box, under **Sort by**, in the first box, select the arrow and select **State** from the list.
    e) Under the first **Then by**, in the first box, choose **City** from the list.
    f) Under the second **Then by**, choose **Zip code**.
    g) Select **OK** to close the dialog box and perform the sort.

3. Verify that the list is sorted by state, city, and then zip code, and then save your changes.

    a) Deselect the text.
    b) Scroll through the list to verify that all of the "CT" entries are listed first, followed by "NY" and then "VT."
    c) Within each of the state groupings, verify that the cities are listed in alphabetical order.
    d) Save your changes.

---

# TOPIC B

## Renumber a List

When you create a numbered list, you may find that you need to add items to it, or that you need to split it into two or more lists. Sometimes, a list has to be interrupted, perhaps to insert additional information under one of the items. Or, the list is getting long and would be easier to follow if split into two lists. Renumbering a list lets you handle such situations without having to retype the list, or cut and paste items into a new list. You can continue numbering after adding extra information into a list, and you can restart numbering in cases where two lists would work better than one.

### Renumbering Options

There are several options to choose from when renumbering a list. On the **HOME** tab, you can turn off list numbering, and turn it back on, by clicking the **Numbering** button. You can also enter an unnumbered item in a numbered list by pressing **Shift+Enter** to start the unnumbered line, and then press **Enter** to continue numbering the list. The **Set Numbering Value** dialog box has options to start a new list, or continue numbering from the previous list. You can open this dialog box by selecting the arrow on the **Numbering** button and choosing **Set Numbering Value** from the list.

 **Access the Checklist tile on your LogicalCHOICE course screen for reference information and job aids on How to Renumber a List**

# ACTIVITY 5-2
## Renumbering a List

### Before You Begin
My Report Draft.docx is open.

### Scenario
In the My Report Draft document, on the second page, another coworker started a list of strategies for membership retention. Some items have had further information added to them. Your manager wants you to add a bit more information to one item in the list, and add an additional list item. You also think the list items fall into two different categories, so you decide to split the list in two. You don't, however, want to have to retype the entire list just for these minor changes. Instead, you'll renumber the list.

1. Scroll to the second page of the document to view the "Membership retention strategies" numbered list.

2. After list item "3. Marketing," add the new piece of information on an unnumbered line.
   a) Click at the end of the list item, and press **Shift+Enter** to create a new, unnumbered line under the list item.
   b) In the new blank line, type *Marketing targeted to older adults tends to increase/retain membership.*

3. Continue the numbering in the list and add a list item after the new informational text.
   a) Press **Enter** to create a new numbered line in the proper sequence.
   b) Type *Free initial fitness evaluation*

4. Split the list into two lists, with the second list beginning under a new heading.
   a) Press **Enter** twice to turn off numbering and move the cursor to the left indent position.
   b) Type *Member incentives*

5. Restart numbering in the second list with the value **1**.
   a) Place the insertion point just before "Availability."
   b) On the **HOME** tab, in the **Paragraph** group, select the arrow on the **Numbering** button and select **Set Numbering Value** to open the **Set Numbering Value** dialog box.
   c) In the dialog box, ensure that **Start new list** is selected, and in the **Set value to** spin box, enter *1*
   d) Select **OK** to close the dialog box and start the new list.

6. Save your changes.

# TOPIC C

## Customize a List

You've created and structured different types of lists. But you might want to take your one-level bulleted or numbered lists to the next step. You may find that you have list items that need their own subsets of information, so you might want to create a list within a list, and apply specific formatting to each level to give special attention to the items therein. You could combine both numbered and bulleted list levels to create a particular focus. Word provides customization options that help you redesign elements of your lists so that certain information is emphasized in a logical manner.

### Multilevel Lists

A *multilevel list*, also known as a sublist, is a list with a hierarchical structure, wherein the number or bullet format is configured separately for each level of the list. You can mix numbers and bullets in multilevel lists. You can demote list items to a lower level by indenting them to the right, so that they can be easily distinguished from higher-level items. A multilevel list can be created from existing content, or you can start one from scratch.

***Member Retention Report***

***Draft outline***

1) Purpose
    a) Determine the best methods for recruitment of new members/retention of current members

2) Procedure
    a) Questionnaires sent to member clubs
        i) Describe current membership recruitment/retention strategies
        ii) Statistics
        iii) Satisfaction ratings from current members

3) Findings
    a) Best strategies for recruitment
        i) Marketing targeted to older adults
        ii) New member incentives

    b) Best Strategies for retention
        i) Intervention
        ii) Meet with member
        iii) Review fitness program and goals
        iv) Loyalty rewards
            - Free month's membership
            - Free apparel item

***Figure 5-1: A multilevel list.***

#### Converting a Numbered List

You can convert a numbered list to a multilevel list by demoting the list items. Word automatically applies the multilevel list format to the new subordinate step.

## List Styles

A list style contains list-specific formatting options for both numbered and bulleted lists. It can be applied to one or more levels of a list. A list style can have up to nine levels, and each level can be individually formatted. You can use Word's built-in list styles, or define a new style with formatting options you choose.

## The Multilevel List Gallery

The **Multilevel List** button in the **Paragraph** group displays a gallery of predefined list styles that can be directly applied to text. The gallery contains up to five sections.

| Section | Description |
|---|---|
| **Current List** | Displays the list style currently in use. |
| **List Library** | Displays predefined list styles. |
| **Lists in Current Documents** | Displays list styles used in other open documents. This section will not appear if no other documents are open. |
| **List Styles** | Displays customized list styles. This section will not appear if no new list styles have been defined. |
| **Other options** | Contains options to create or modify list levels and styles. |

### Define New Multilevel List vs. Define New List Style

The **Define New Multilevel List** command is used when you create and save a list style that won't be changed, or that you will use in a single document. The **Define New List Style** command is used to change a style design.

 **Access the Checklist tile on your LogicalCHOICE course screen for reference information and job aids on How to Create a Multilevel List**

# ACTIVITY 5–3
## Creating a Multilevel List

### Before You Begin
My Report Draft.docx is open.

### Scenario
In anticipation of creating the Member Retention Report, a coworker has entered a list of report elements, but they are all the same level and it's hard to distinguish the topics from the subtopics. You want to help shape the list so that it begins to look more organized. You decide to convert the single-level list into a multilevel list, so that it looks like the right side of the following graphic.

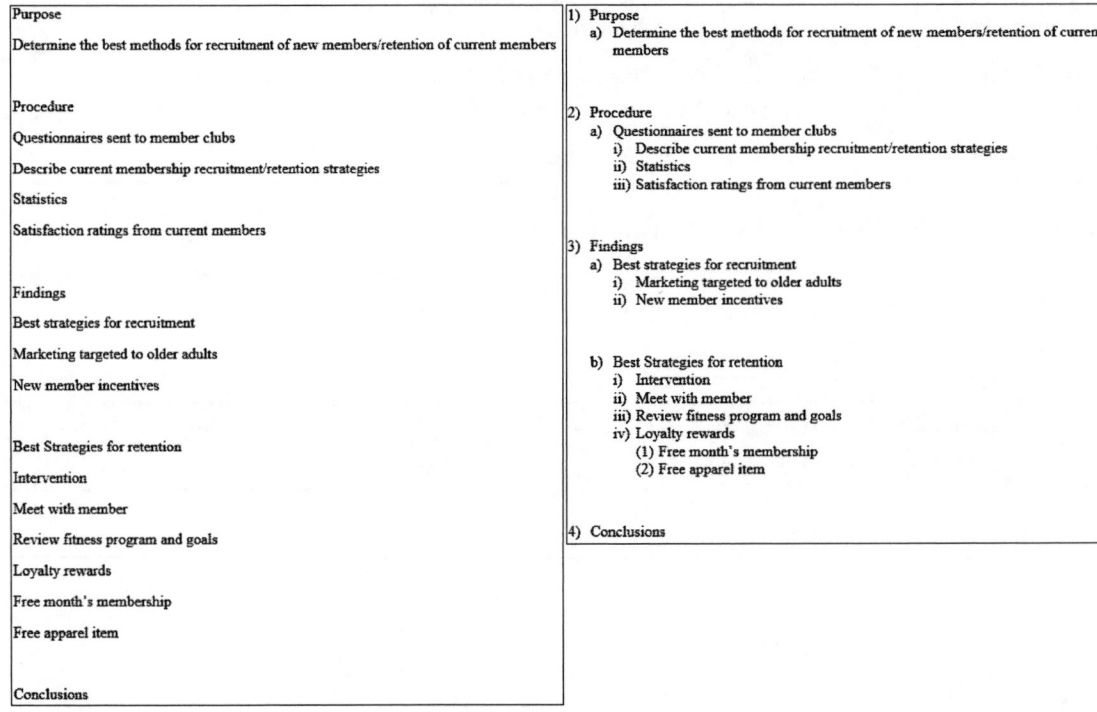

1. Create a multilevel list from the existing list items on page 3 of the document.
   a) Navigate to page 3 of the document.
   b) Under **Draft outline**, select all the list items.

    **Note:** You might want to adjust the **Zoom** level so that you can see the entire list on your screen to make it easier to work with the list.

   c) On the **HOME** tab, in the **Paragraph** group, select the **Multilevel List** button to open the **Multilevel List** gallery.
   d) In the **List Library**, select the first multilevel list style to the right of **None**.

2. Apply the second list level to list items **2**, **4**, **9**, and **12**.

   a) Select list item **2**, then press **Ctrl** and select items **4**, **9**, and **12**.

1) Purpose
2) Determine the best methods for recruitment of new members/retention of current members

3) Procedure
4) Questionnaires sent to member clubs
5) Describe current membership recruitment/retention strategies
6) Statistics
7) Satisfaction ratings from current members

8) Findings
9) Best strategies for recruitment
10) Marketing targeted to older adults
11) New member incentives

12) Best Strategies for retention
13) Intervention
14) Meet with member

   b) On the **HOME** tab, in the **Paragraph** group, click the **Increase Indent** button once to demote the selected items. Note that the list items have been renumbered.

3. Demote list items to the third list level.
   a) Select the list items **3-5**, **7-8**, and **9-12**.

   1) Purpose
     a) Determine the best methods for recruitment of new members/retention of current members

   2) Procedure
     a) Questionnaires sent to member clubs
   3) Describe current membership recruitment/retention strategies
   4) Statistics
   5) Satisfaction ratings from current members

   6) Findings
     a) Best strategies for recruitment
   7) Marketing targeted to older adults
   8) New member incentives

     a) Best Strategies for retention
   9) Intervention
   10) Meet with member
   11) Review fitness program and goals
   12) Loyalty rewards

   b) Press **Tab** twice.

4. Demote the list items **4** and **5** to the fourth list level.
   a) Select list items **4** and **5**.
   b) On the **HOME** tab, in the **Paragraph** group, select the arrow on the **Multilevel List** button, select **Change List Level**, and select **Level 4**, the fourth in the list.

3) Findings
   a) Best strategies for recruitment
      i)   Marketing targeted to older adults
      ii)  New member incentives

   b) Best Strategies for retention
      i)   Intervention
      ii)  Meet with member
      iii) Review fitness program and goals
      iv)  Loyalty rewards
           (1) Free month's membership
           (2) Free apparel item

5. Save your changes.

## List Appearance Customization Options

Based on the list type you use, you are presented with a variety of options to choose from for customizing the appearance of your list.

| List Type | Customization Options |
| --- | --- |
| Bulleted list | You can set a symbol, picture, or font as the bullet character. The **Define New Bullet** dialog box contains options that control the choice of symbol or picture used as the bullet, and the font from which the bullet can be selected. You can also set left, center, or right alignment options for the bullet. |
| Numbered list | You can set different number styles or fonts as the number format for a list. The **Define New Number Format** dialog box controls the style of numbering (Arabic numerals, Roman numerals, letters, and so on) and the font from which the numbers are selected. You can also set left, center, or right alignment options for the numbers. |
| Multilevel list | The **Change List Level** options enable you to change the list levels for a multilevel list. The action will be applied on the selected item in the multilevel list only. You can set the spacing between the bullet and the list item. In the **Define New Multilevel List** dialog box, the **Text indent at** spin box controls the amount of space between the bullet or number and the text in the list item. You can also customize your list by using the **Define New List Style** dialog box. The list you customize will appear in the **Multilevel List** gallery. |

 **Access the Checklist tile on your LogicalCHOICE course screen for reference information and job aids on How to Customize List Appearance**

# ACTIVITY 5-4
## Customizing a List's Appearance

### Before You Begin

My Report Draft.docx is open.

### Scenario

There are a couple of modifications you'd like to make to the multilevel list. You don't think the level 4 items should be in a hierarchical format, as both items are equally important, so you decide to convert them to a bulleted format. But, you also want to be sure they don't get lost in the list, so you'll customize the bullets to make the items stand out a little better.

1. Convert the fourth-level list items to a bulleted list.

   a) Select **Free month's membership** and **Free apparel item** at the fourth level in the list.

   b) On the **HOME** tab, in the **Paragraph** group, select the **Bullets** button to convert the items to a bulleted list.

2. Create a new bullet style and apply it to the bulleted list.

   a) On the **Bullets** button, select the arrow, and select **Define New Bullet** to open the **Define New Bullet** dialog box.

   b) In the dialog box, select **Symbol** to display a list of symbols.

   c) In the list, select the right-pointing arrow.

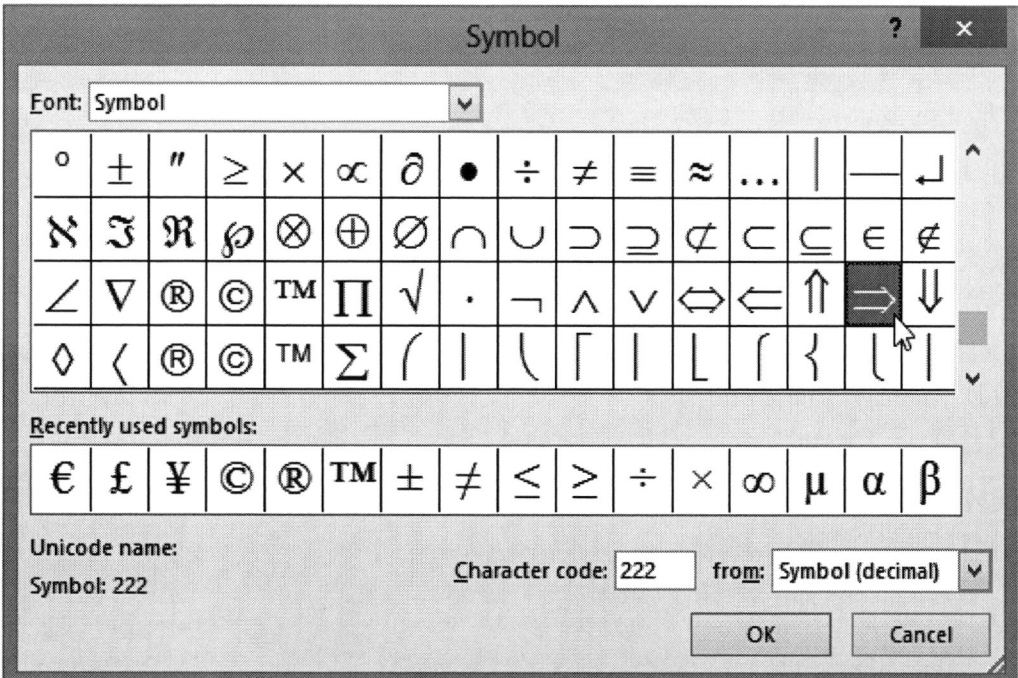

   d) Select **OK** to close the **Symbol** dialog box.

   e) Select **OK** to close the **Define New Bullet** dialog box and apply the new style.

   f) Deselect the text.

b) Best Strategies for retention
   i) Intervention
   ii) Meet with member
   iii) Review fitness program and goals
   iv) Loyalty rewards
       ⇒ Free month's membership
       ⇒ Free apparel item

3. Save your changes, and close the document.

# Summary

In this lesson, you managed different types of lists using a variety of techniques. Because lists are such a common element in Word documents, knowing how to control and enhance them will help you to present information in a more organized and visually appealing way.

**In what way will the ability to sort information help you with your work responsibilities?**

**When might you want to use a multilevel list?**

> **Note:** Check your LogicalCHOICE Course screen for opportunities to interact with your classmates, peers, and the larger LogicalCHOICE online community about the topics covered in this course or other topics you are interested in. From the Course screen you can also access available resources for a more continuous learning experience.

# 6 | Inserting Graphic Objects

**Lesson Time: 20 minutes**

## Lesson Objectives

In this lesson, you will:

- Insert symbols and special characters.

- Add images to a document.

## Lesson Introduction

One way to add some sparkle to your Microsoft® Word 2013 documents is by using graphics, whether to present information in a dramatic way, to "brand" your documents with a company logo, or just to add color and variety. Pictures, illustrations, symbols, and special characters can add a fresh layer of interest to your documents.

Think about a time when you had to read a lengthy document that contained only text. Even if the content was well organized and readable, it probably got a little boring after awhile. While graphics aren't always appropriate in certain types of documents, they will add interest if used wisely.

# TOPIC A

## Insert Symbols and Special Characters

You've applied various formatting techniques to enhance the appearance of text. Certain terms, however, require special handling in order to explain exactly what they are. You probably wouldn't describe the price of something as simply "10." Your reader would wonder: "Ten what?" To clarify, you'd add the $ symbol. The $ symbol and a few others are easy to insert because they appear right on the keyboard. But what about other common symbols and special characters? Ever wonder how to type the registered trademark character ®? It's not on the typical keyboard. Fortunately, Word provides convenient access to a large group of such symbols and special characters.

## Symbols

*Symbols* are characters used to represent an idea or a word, such as copyright, trademark, or registered trademark. They can be mathematical operators, currency symbols, geometric shapes, or supplemental punctuation marks. They can be emoticons, or characters from foreign languages.

You can insert symbols using several methods.

- On the **INSERT** tab, select **Symbol**.
- In the **Symbol** dialog box, select a symbol.
- Press the key combination associated with some of the symbols.
- Define a key combination for inserting symbols you often use.

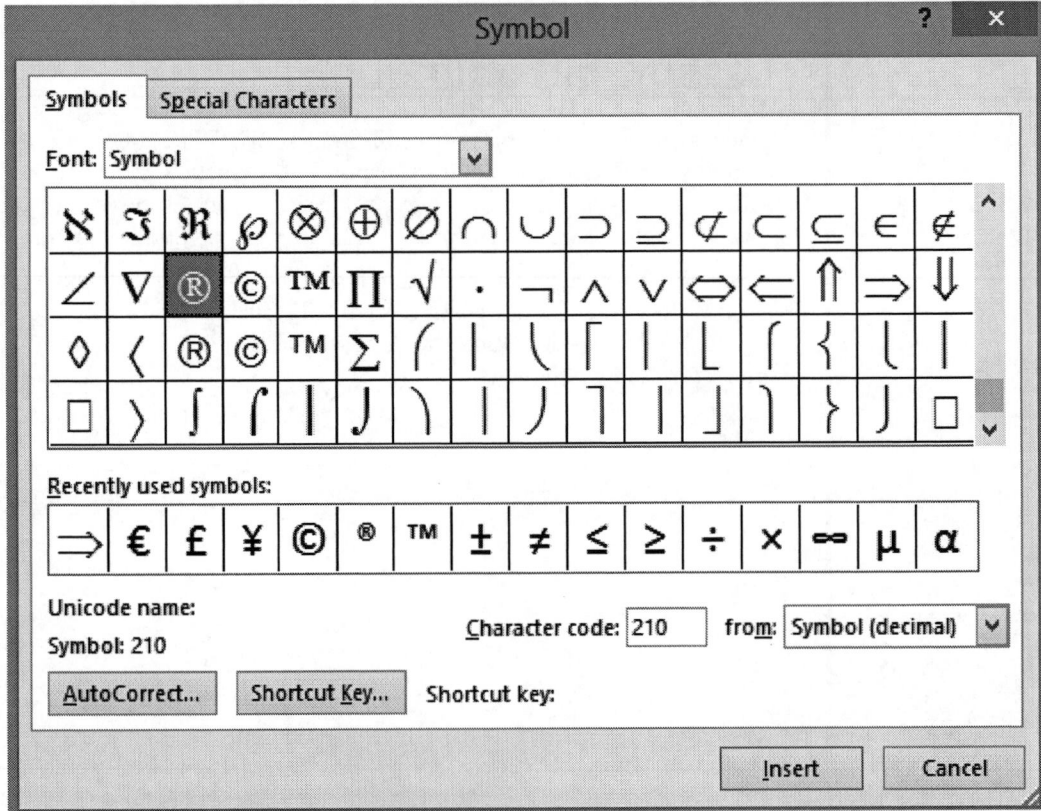

*Figure 6-1: Different symbols available in Word.*

## The Wingdings Font

Wingdings is a font available in Word that includes many decorative symbols. Wingdings characters include familiar objects such as "smileys," as well as other whimsical and useful symbols.

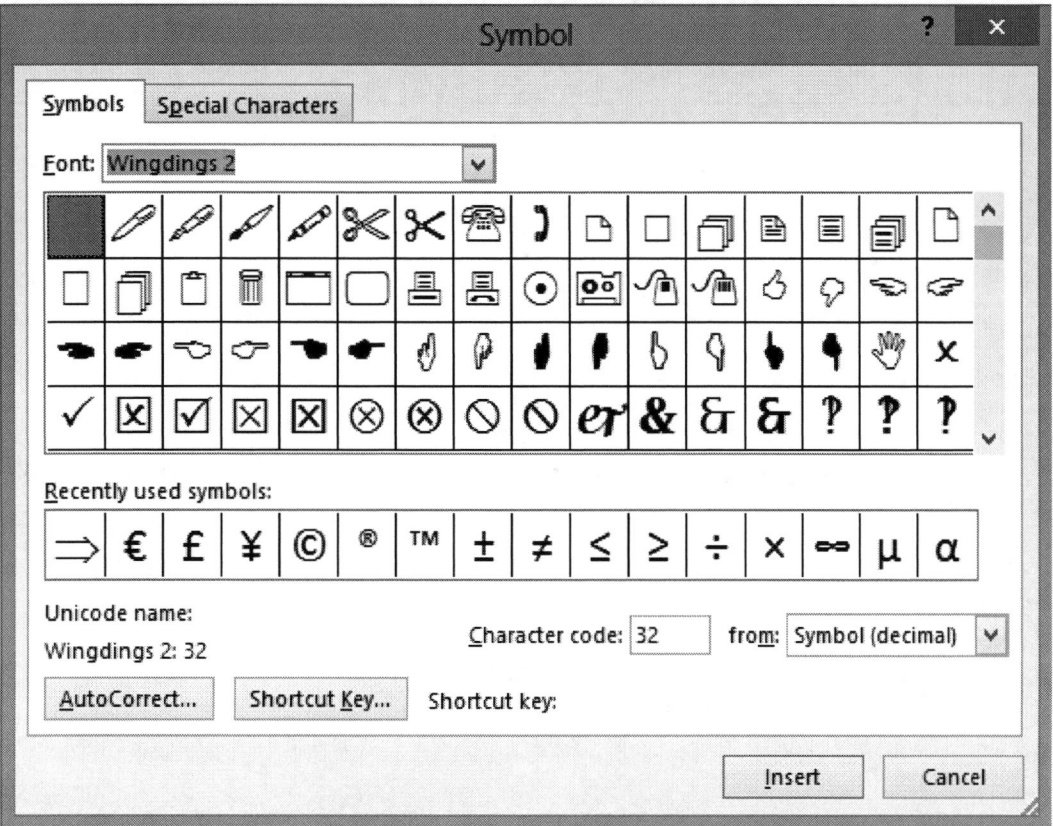

*Figure 6-2: Wingdings Fonts are available in the Symbols dialog box.*

# Special Characters

*Special characters* include punctuation, spacing, or typographical characters that typically are not available on a standard keyboard. Ellipses ( … ) or em dashes ( — ) are examples of special characters. Some special characters, like © and ®, are also symbols. Most special characters can be inserted with a predefined key combination, or you can create your own key combination to insert a character.

 **Access the Checklist tile on your LogicalCHOICE course screen for reference information and job aids on How to Insert Symbols and Special Characters**

# ACTIVITY 6-1
## Inserting Symbols and Special Characters in a Document

### Data Files

C:\091024Data\Inserting Graphic Objects\Bit by Bit Fitness Draft.docx

### Scenario

You've noticed that the Bit by Bit Fitness draft document is missing some needed special characters to denote registered trademark names. You'd also like to add symbols to the list of amenities to draw the readers' attention to it.

---

1. Navigate to the **C:\091024Data\Inserting Graphic Objects** folder, open **Bit by Bit Fitness Draft.docx**, and save it as *My Bit by Bit Fitness Draft.docx*

2. On the first page of the document, find the first instance of "Zumba," and add the ® special character after the word.
   a) Place the insertion point after the word **Zumba** but before the comma.
   b) On the **INSERT** tab, in the **Symbols** group, select **Symbol** to open the **Symbols** gallery.
   c) In the gallery, select the ® character to insert it.
      If the ® character was found in the **Symbols** gallery, continue to Step 4; if it wasn't found continue with sub-step d.
   d) If the character doesn't appear in the gallery, select **More Symbols** to open the **Symbol** dialog box.
   e) On the **Special Characters** tab, select the **Registered** special character.

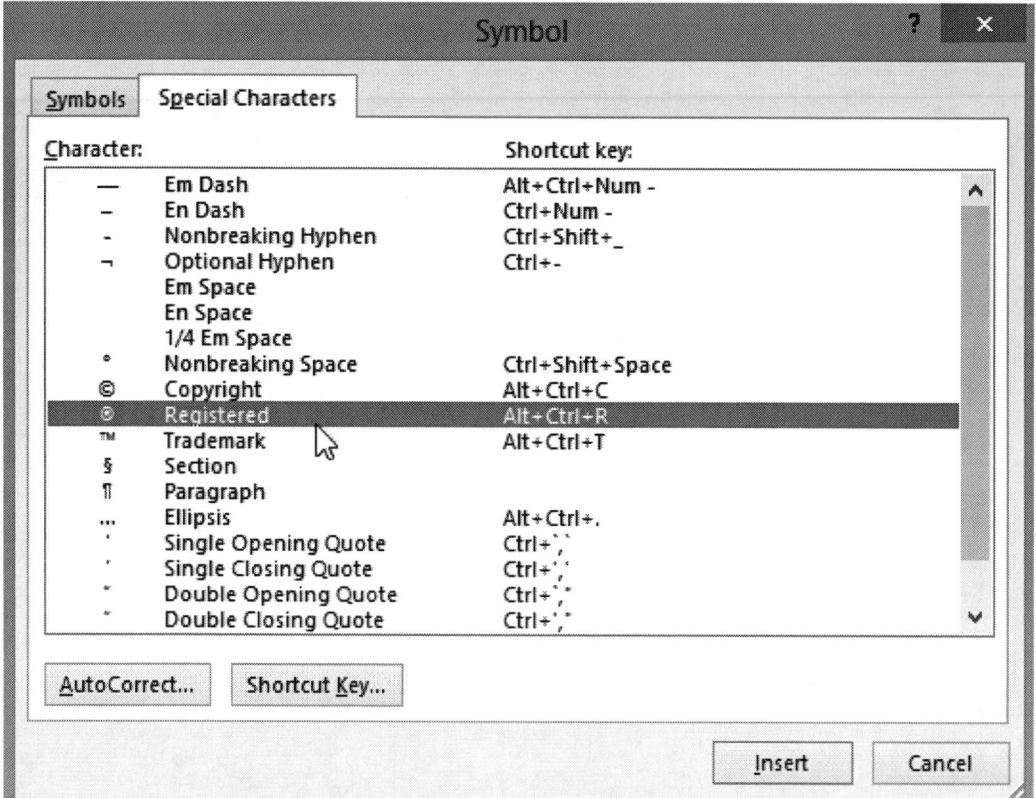

f) Select **Insert** to insert the character.

g) Select **Close** to close the dialog box.

3. Insert the **Registered** special character after the second instance of "Zumba."

   a) On the second page, under the "What We Offer" heading, place the insertion point after the word **Zumba** but before the comma.

   b) Press **Ctrl+Y** to repeat the last action.

4. Under "What We Offer," insert a check mark symbol before the items in the list.

   a) Place the insertion point just before "Cardiovascular Equipment."

   b) Select **Symbol→More Symbols** to open the **Symbol** dialog box.

   c) On the **Symbol** tab, in the **Font** list, select **Wingdings 2**.

   d) If necessary, scroll through the **Wingdings 2** gallery, and select the **check mark** symbol. Or, in the **Character code** text box, type *80* to find and select the **check mark** symbol.

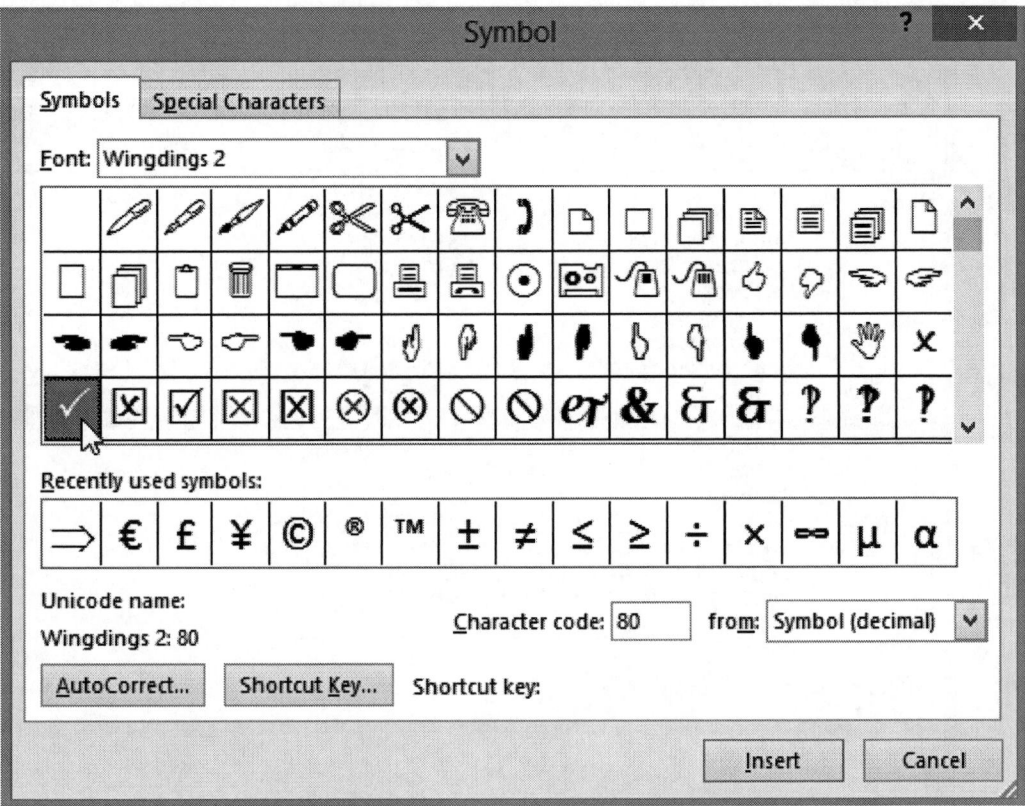

e) Select **Insert** to insert the symbol.
f) Select **Close**.
g) Add the symbol to the remaining list items.

5. Save your changes.

# TOPIC B

## Add Images to a Document

Have you ever read a travel brochure that didn't contain pictures? Probably not. A travel agency wouldn't generate much interest in special deals to faraway places without pictures to spark the imagination. Brochures, flyers, web pages, and even business reports are all enhanced by the inclusion of pictures and other graphical objects. With Word, you can add pictures, illustrations, and clip art to draw your readers' attention and accentuate your message.

## Illustrations

An illustration is a graphical object used to explain or embellish text. In Word, illustrations include pictures, clip art, shapes, SmartArt, charts, and screenshots. After you insert an illustration in a Word document, you can move, resize, or apply various other formatting options to it.

### SmartArt

SmartArt graphics are graphic elements that combine text, illustrations, and color. They can be used to create diagrams, and organization and flow charts.

### Charts

A chart is a graphical representation of statistical data. Charts are used to visually represent a relationship between different groups of data. Different types of charts include bar, pie, and line.

## Pictures

In Word, a picture generally refers to a photographic image, or other type of image that closely resembles a real object. Pictures are most often stored as JPEG, PNG, or GIF files, which are file formats used to organize or store images. Word comes with a few pre-installed sample pictures, and you can download more at Office.com.

## Clip Art

Clip art is a term that, at one time, generally referred to non-photographic images. Currently, however, it can include various types of ready-made graphics. In Word, you can access clip art on Office.com.

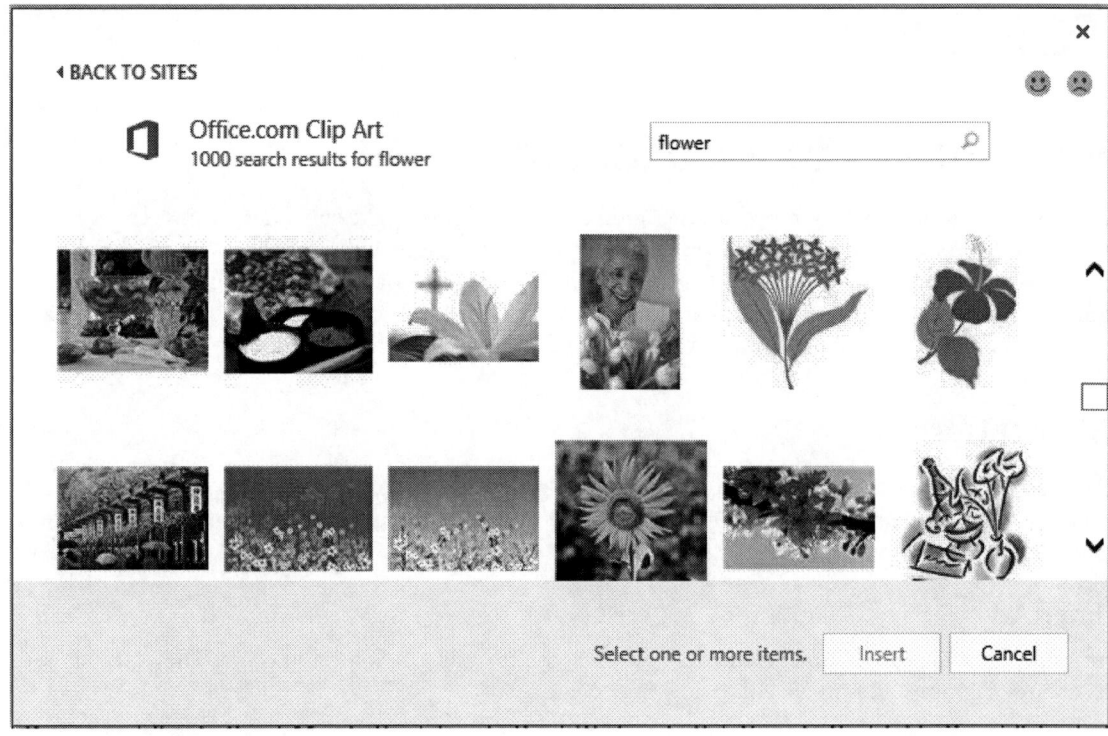

*Figure 6-3: Clip art graphics of flowers.*

## The PICTURE TOOLS FORMAT Contextual Tab

You can use the **PICTURE TOOLS FORMAT** contextual tab to position, resize, and apply various styles and effects to illustrations in a document. The groups on the contextual tab help you adjust your picture in several ways.

| Group | Helps You |
|---|---|
| **Adjust** | Format images by increasing or decreasing the color, brightness, or contrast. |
| **Picture Styles** | Select a style, shape, border, and effect for a picture. |
| **Arrange** | Position an image in the document. By using the options in this group, you can also rotate, group, or align the pictures within a page. |
| **Size** | Crop an image and increase or decrease its height and width. |

 **Access the Checklist tile on your LogicalCHOICE course screen for reference information and job aids on How to Add Images to a Document**

# ACTIVITY 6-2
## Adding an Image to a Document

### Data Files

C:\091024Data\Inserting Graphic Objects\logo.png

### Before You Begin

My Bit by Bit Fitness Draft.docx is open.

### Scenario

In looking over the Bit by Bit Fitness draft document, you realize that inserting the company logo would add some appropriate color and interest, as well as add a "branding" element that immediately identifies which company the document belongs to.

---

1. Add **logo.png** to the beginning of the document.
   a) Position the insertion point at the top of the document.
   b) On the **INSERT** tab, in the **Illustrations** group, select **Pictures** to open the **Insert Picture** dialog box.
   c) Navigate to the **C:\091024Data\Inserting Graphic Objects** folder, and select **logo.png**.
   d) Select **Insert**.

2. Position the logo to the right of the first line in the document.
   a) On the **PICTURE TOOLS FORMAT** contextual tab, in the **Arrange** group, select **Position** to open the **Object Position** gallery.
   b) Select the **Position in Top Right with Square Text Wrapping** option.

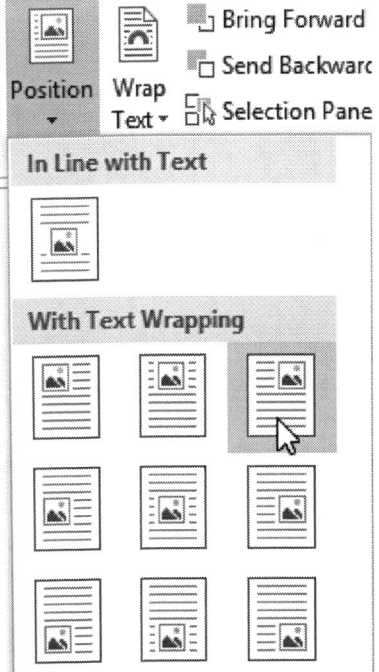

3. Deselect the picture.

4. Insert a clip art image about fitness.
   a) Position the insertion point at the end of the document.
   b) Select **INSERT→Online Pictures**.
   c) In the **Insert Pictures** dialog box, in the **Office.com Clip Art** text box, type *fitness* and then click the **Search** button.
   d) Select an appropriate image and then select **Insert**.

5. Save your changes and then close the document.

# Summary

In this lesson, you inserted graphical objects into a document. Symbols, special characters, and illustrations can boost the visual appeal of your documents, and help convey information more dramatically than simple text.

**Which symbols and special characters do you think you'll use most often during the course of your work?**

**How do you intend to use illustrations in your documents?**

 **Note:** Check your LogicalCHOICE Course screen for opportunities to interact with your classmates, peers, and the larger LogicalCHOICE online community about the topics covered in this course or other topics you are interested in. From the Course screen you can also access available resources for a more continuous learning experience.

# 7 Controlling Page Appearance

**Lesson Time: 30 minutes**

## Lesson Objectives

In this lesson, you will:

- Apply page borders and colors.

- Apply a watermark.

- Add a header and footer to a document.

- Control the layout of a page.

## Lesson Introduction

You've applied formatting options and inserted illustrations and other elements that boost the readability of the text in your document. You can also configure other formatting options to alter the appearance of the pages themselves. Fine-tuning a Microsoft® Word 2013 page can mean adding design elements that help give either a more professional look or an informal feel, depending on your intent. Layout options can determine how text and graphics flow on the page.

# TOPIC A

## Apply a Page Border and Color

In addition to adding borders and colors to paragraphs and tables, Word allows you to apply these elements to an entire page. This is useful for when you want to give your document a polished, or even whimsical look. Documents such as invitations or certificates might be enhanced by decorative borders, or perhaps a subtle color choice to amplify the text on the page. Business documents might be more visually interesting with an understated border. Word provides many choices for page borders and colors, and you can apply them with a few simple clicks.

### Page Borders

A page border frames the page of a document. Page borders can be simple or decorative, with a variety of styles, colors, and widths. Borders can be applied to the document as a whole, to a specific section, the first page only, or all pages except the first page. Page borders in Word have two different types of lines: straight lines of various styles and widths, and artistic styles, consisting of small decorative elements. The straight-line type is the Word default, and is more appropriate for business reports or academic papers. Art borders can enliven less formal documents, such as invitations, certificates, and cards.

### Border Options

You can select various options for your page borders on the **Page Border** tab of the **Borders and Shading** dialog box. Here, you can set the border type, and the line style, color, and width. You can choose an **Art** border from a gallery of graphical elements. The **Preview** pane on the **Page Border** tab allows you see what your border options will look like before they are applied. You can choose to apply the border to every page, or only certain pages.

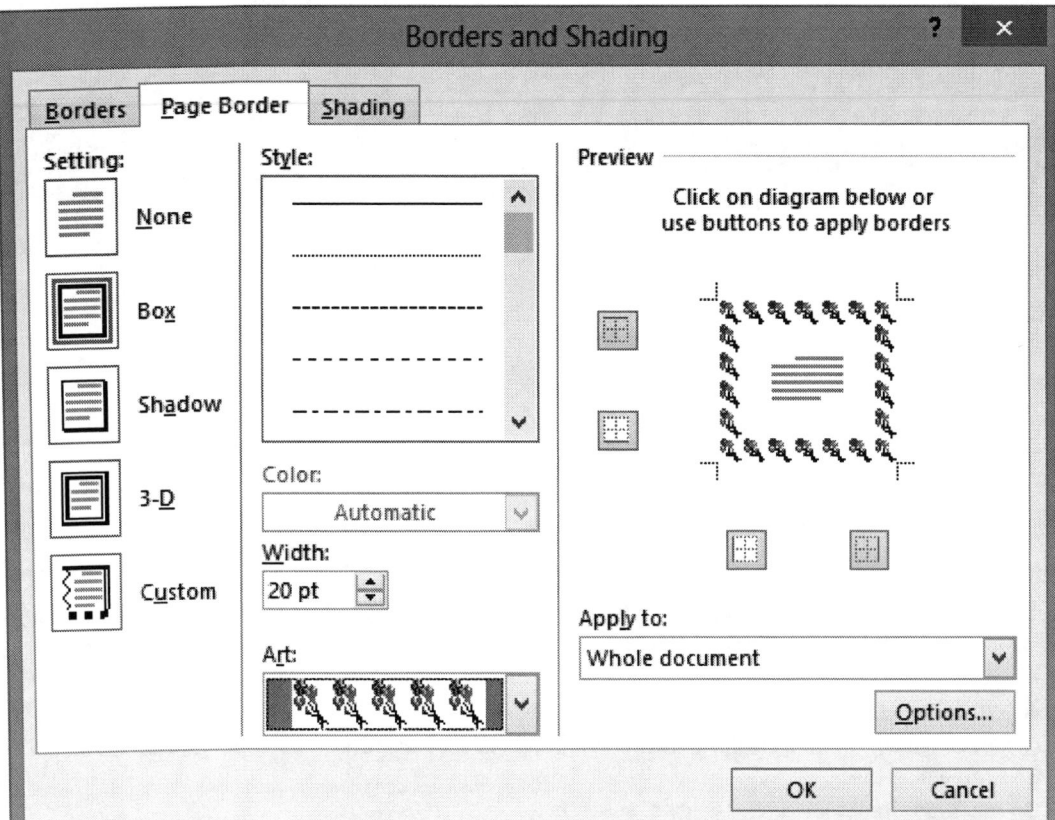

*Figure 7-1: Page Border tab showing a preview of an Art border.*

## Page Color Options

Page colors can be applied to the background of a page. You can select a color from the **Page Color** gallery, or define a custom color. In addition, you can create different effects with gradient, texture, or pattern choices by using the **Fill Effects** dialog box in the **Page Color** gallery. You can even define a picture as a page background.

 **Note:** To further learn about applying page colors, you can access the LearnTO **Apply a Page Color** presentation from the **LearnTO** tile on the LogicalCHOICE Course screen.

### Printing Backgrounds

By default, Word doesn't preview or print background colors. You need to enable this feature in the **Word Options** dialog box, on the **Display** tab, by checking the **Print background colors and images** check box.

 Access the Checklist tile on your LogicalCHOICE course screen for reference information and job aids on How to Apply Page Borders and Colors

# ACTIVITY 7–1
## Applying a Page Border

### Data Files

C:\091024Data\Controlling Page Appearance\Bit by Bit Fitness Draft.docx

### Scenario

You wonder whether a page border might be appropriate for a business-oriented document. It might add a bit of distinction to the pages, but you think it should be very subtle, so as not to distract from the document content. You decide to apply a light page border to increase the visual interest of the document pages.

---

1. Navigate to the **C:\091024Data\Controlling Page Appearance** folder, open **Bit by Bit Fitness Draft.docx**, and save it as *My Bit by Bit Fitness Draft.docx*

2. Apply a page border to the document.
   a) On the **DESIGN** tab, in the **Page Background** group, select **Page Borders** to open the **Borders and Shading** dialog box.
   b) On the **Page Border** tab, under **Setting**, select **Box**.
   c) In the **Style** list, select the first dotted-line style.
   d) In the **Color** list, select the **White, Background 1, Darker 25%** color swatch.
   e) Select **OK**.

3. Save your changes.

---

# TOPIC B

## Add a Watermark

You've configured page borders, and learned about adding color to the background of your document. There are other background elements you can add that are very useful in identifying the type of document you're working on, or the type of information it contains. Often, you'll want to designate a particular document as a work in progress, or as containing confidential information that isn't to be shared publicly. You could put such information in the content of the document, but it might be overlooked. Word allows you to insert a watermark in the background of a document, to clearly identify the uses to which the document can be put.

## Watermarks

A watermark is transparent text or a graphic that appears in the background of a document. It is generally used to designate the purpose or content of a document, or to prove authenticity in an unmistakable way. Watermarks are often applied to prevent copyright infringement or intellectual property theft. Once you add a watermark, it is automatically applied to the whole document. You can apply a watermark quickly by using the built-in watermarks from the **Watermark** gallery, accessible on the **DESIGN** tab, in the **Page Background** group, by selecting the **Watermark** button. Or, you can customize a watermark by using the **Printed Watermark** dialog box.

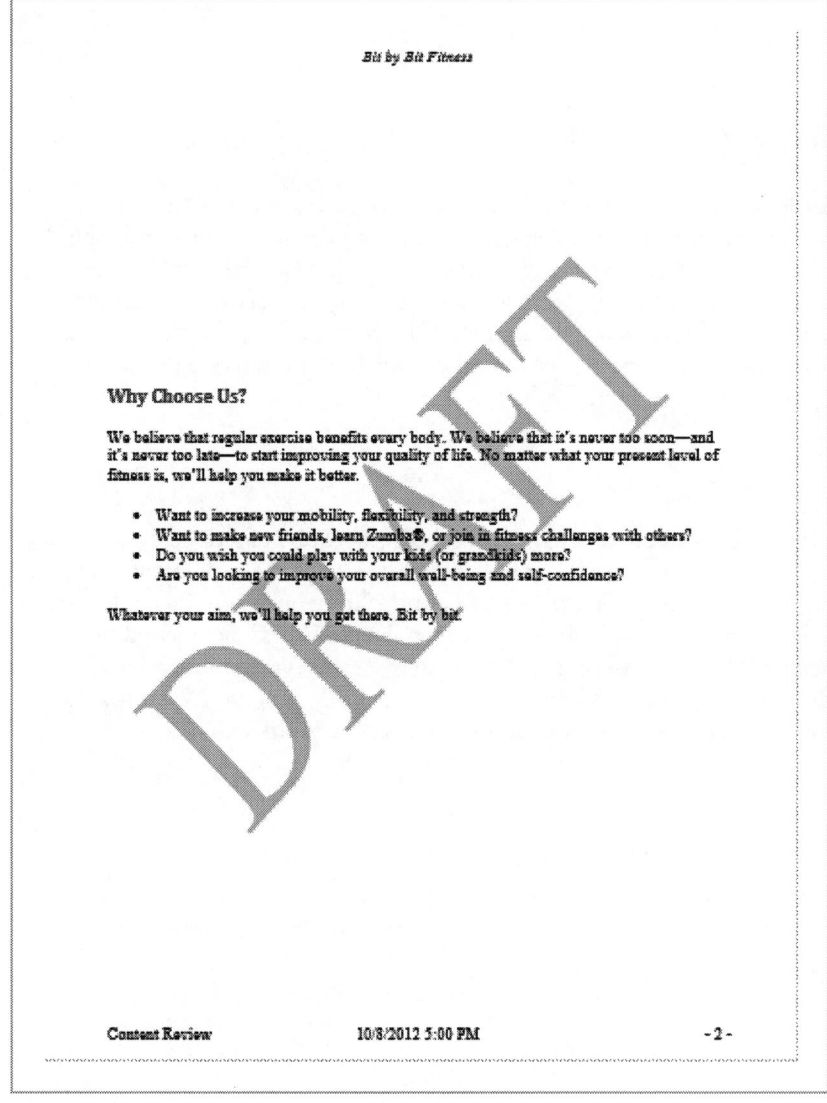

*Figure 7–2: A watermark for a draft document.*

## The Printed Watermark Dialog Box

In Word, when you want a custom watermark, you can use the **Printed Watermark** dialog box. To access this dialog box go to the **DESIGN** tab, in the **Page Background** group, select the **Watermark** button and then select **Custom Watermark** from the list. You can select a picture to use as a watermark, scale the picture, and adjust its transparency. Or, you can select a text watermark, and configure font, size, color, and layout of the text. You can also use the **Printed Watermark** dialog box to remove a watermark.

 Access the Checklist tile on your LogicalCHOICE course screen for reference information and job aids on How to Add a Watermark

# ACTIVITY 7-2
## Adding a Watermark to a Document

### Before You Begin
My Bit by Bit Fitness Draft.docx is open.

### Scenario
Although the title of the document you've been working on includes the word "Draft," it's possible someone might mistake it for the final version. One way to make sure this doesn't happen is to add a watermark that leaves no doubt in the readers' minds about the version of the document. You decide to add a watermark that clearly identifies that the document is a draft.

1. Insert a custom text watermark.
   a) On the **DESIGN** tab, in the **Page Background** group, select **Watermark** to open the **Watermark** gallery.
   b) From the gallery, select **Custom Watermark** to open the **Printed Watermark** dialog box.
   c) In the dialog box, select **Text watermark**.
   d) From the **Text** list, select **DRAFT**.
   e) From the **Font** list, if necessary, select **Times New Roman**.
   f) Select **OK**.

2. Preview the document.
   a) Select **FILE→Print**.
   b) Notice that the word "Draft" appears across the page.
   c) Select the **Back** button.

3. Save your changes.

# TOPIC C

## Add Headers and Footers

Watermarks are one way to add identifying details to the pages of a document. Another way to provide useful, repeating information in a document is to add headers and footers.

Did you ever drop an unbound, multi-page document, and watch the pages scatter? As you put the pages back in order, you were probably thankful that each page was numbered. Perhaps your document also had an author name and title listed at the top or bottom of each page, identifying which document the pages belonged to. Such information also helps you navigate more easily through an electronic document, and provides a professional look. Typing this information on each individual page would be a tedious and time-consuming task. Fortunately, you only need to add it once, in a header or footer.

## Headers and Footers

*Headers* and *footers* are defined areas at the top and the bottom margins of a page where you can add textual or graphical information that is common to all or to some of the pages in a document. Common information such as titles, dates, and page numbers can be entered in the left, center, or right sections of a header and footer. You can specify whether headers and footers should appear on the first page of the document. You can also apply different header and footer content to odd and even numbered pages.

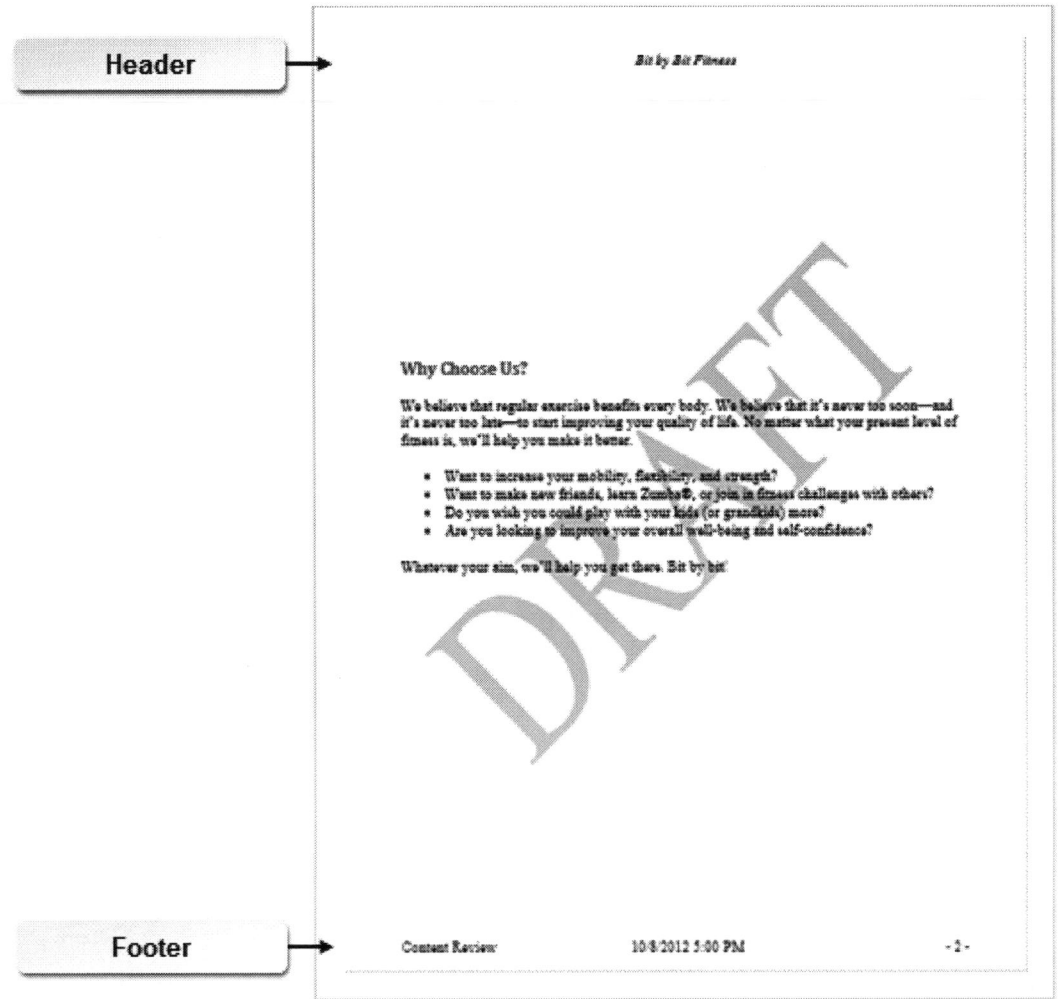

*Figure 7-3: A header and footer.*

### Fields

When you add content to a header or footer, Word inserts a *field* for each item of information. A field is a placeholder for a certain type of data. If you've ever filled out a tax or employment form, you know that your name goes into a name field, the date goes into a date field, and so on. You can configure certain fields to update automatically, which can be especially useful when, for example, you want to show the current date and time in a document.

## The HEADER & FOOTER TOOLS DESIGN Contextual Tab

The **HEADER & FOOTER TOOLS DESIGN** contextual tab opens when you insert a header or footer. Use the groups on the tab to help you work with headers and footers.

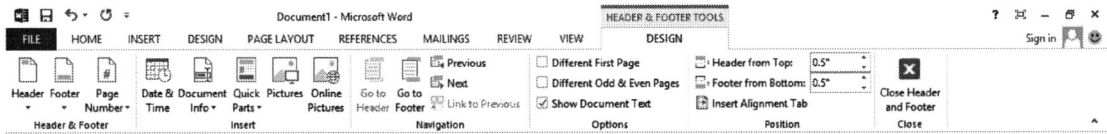

*Figure 7-4: The HEADER & FOOTER TOOLS DESIGN contextual tab.*

| Group | Description |
|---|---|
| **Header & Footer** | Contains built-in styles for headers, footers, and page numbers, as well as options to edit or remove these elements. |
| **Insert** | Contains options that enable you to insert objects, such as pictures and clip art images, in headers and footers. You can also insert a date and time field. |
| **Navigation** | Contains options to navigate to a header, footer, and previous or next sections in a document. |
| **Options** | Contains options to apply different formatting to the header or footer on the first page, on odd and even pages, or to the entire document. |
| **Position** | Contains options to modify the size, or margins, of the header and footer area. This group also allows you to align the content of the header and footer. |
| **Close** | Allows you to close the header or footer section and return to the normal view of the document. |

 **Access the Checklist tile on your LogicalCHOICE course screen for reference information and job aids on How to Insert and Delete Headers and Footers**

# ACTIVITY 7–3
## Inserting Headers and Footers

### Before You Begin
My Bit by Bit Fitness Draft.docx is open.

### Scenario
You'd like a coworker to go over the information in your document and offer suggestions. First, though, you want to make sure that the pages contain some identifying information, such as the company name, the document's purpose, the page order, and the current date and time. In this activity, you'll add a header and footer to the document to contain this information.

1. Insert and center the text "Bit by Bit Fitness" into the header of the document.
   a) Double-click near the top of any page to display the header and footer areas.
   b) Press **Tab** to center-align the insertion point.
   c) Type *Bit by Bit Fitness*

2. Insert the built-in footer style **Blank (Three Columns)**.
   a) On the **HEADER & FOOTER TOOLS DESIGN** contextual tab, in the **Header & Footer** group, select **Footer** to open the **Footer** gallery.
   b) From the gallery, select **Blank (Three Columns)**.

3. Insert the text **Content Review** in the first column of the footer.
   a) Click within the brackets of the first footer column to select it, and type *Content Review*

4. Insert the current date and time in the second column of the footer, and set it to update automatically.
   a) Select the second footer column.
   b) In the **Insert** group, select **Date & Time**.
   c) In the **Date and Time** dialog box, select the date and time format shown.

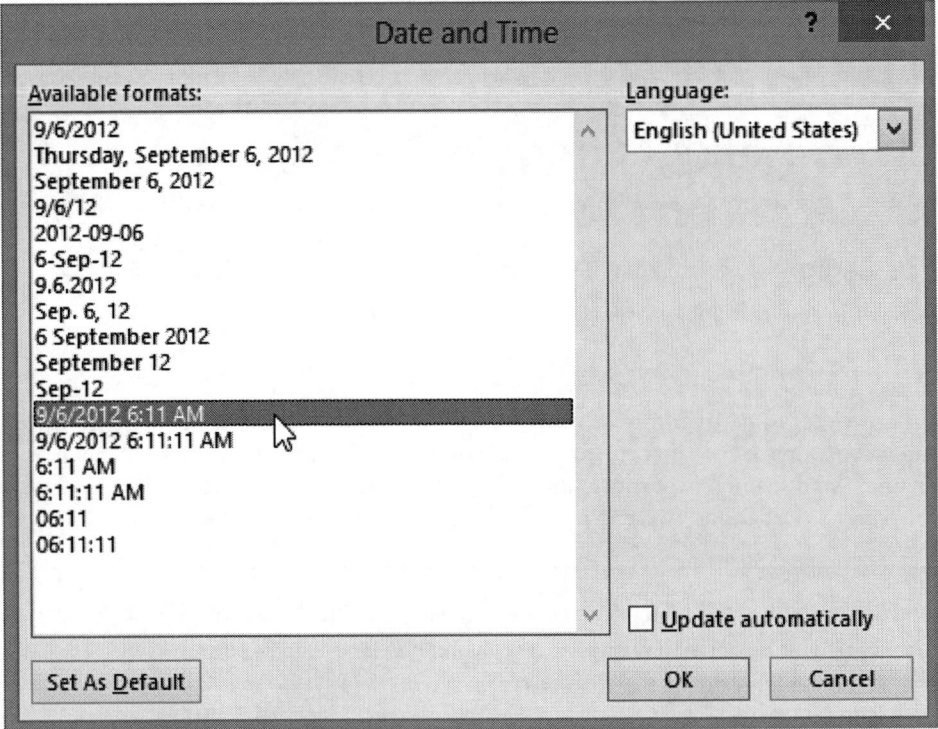

d) Check the **Update automatically** check box.

e) Select **OK** to insert the date and time.

5. Insert a page number in the third column of the footer.

a) Select the third footer column.

b) In the **Header & Footer** group, select **Page Number**.

c) From the gallery, select **Current Position→Plain Number**.

6. Preview the document.

7. Save your changes.

---

 Access the Checklist tile on your LogicalCHOICE course screen for reference information and job aids on How to Modify Headers and Footers

# ACTIVITY 7-4
## Modifying a Header and Footer

### Before You Begin
My Bit by Bit Fitness Draft.docx is open.

### Scenario
You've inserted a header and footer in your document, but you don't like either appearing on the first page. You also think the page numbers should stand out a little more, and that the text in the header would look better italicized. You decide to modify the header and footer.

1. Convert the page numbers to a different format.
   a) If necessary, double-click near the bottom of the first page to open the footer.
   b) On the **HEADER & FOOTER TOOLS DESIGN** contextual tab, in the **Header & Footer** group, select **Page Number** to open the **Page Number** gallery.
   c) In the gallery, select **Format Page Numbers** to open the **Page Number Format** dialog box.
   d) From the **Number format** list, select the with numbers and dashes.

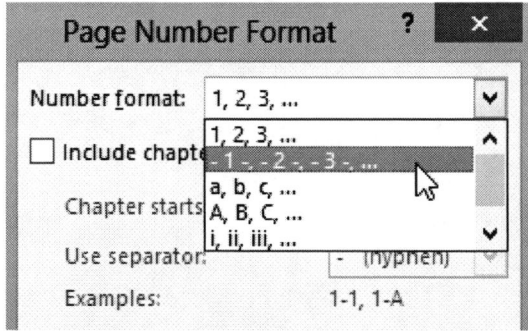

   e) Select **OK**.

2. Italicize the header text.
   a) On the **HEADER & FOOTER TOOLS DESIGN** contextual tab, in the **Navigation** group, select **Go to Header**.
   b) Select the header text, and press **Ctrl+I**.

3. Configure the header and footer so that they don't appear on the first page of the document.
   a) On the **HEADER & FOOTER TOOLS DESIGN** contextual tab, in the **Options** group, check **Different First Page**.

4. Preview the document.

5. Save your changes.

# TOPIC D

## Control Page Layout

Adjusting the overall page layout allows you to fine-tune the appearance of your document before it's printed. Often, the way a document displays on a screen is not the way you'll want it to look when printed. You may want to enlarge the area where text can go, or create more white space in the document to facilitate reading. Perhaps you're printing a certificate of achievement to honor an employee's completion of a work project. You'd probably want to adjust the document orientation so that it resembles a conventional certificate. Defining page layout options helps harmonize the flow of text and graphics on the page.

## Margin Options

A margin refers to the area between the edge of a page and the place where text begins. Generally, you insert text between page margins, although some page elements, like headers and footers, occupy the margin area. You have many options for defining page margins in Word. You can apply a predefined margin type, or you can create custom margins. You apply margin options via the **Margins** gallery, accessible from the **Page Setup** group of the **PAGE LAYOUT** tab. You can also apply custom margins from the **Page Setup** dialog box.

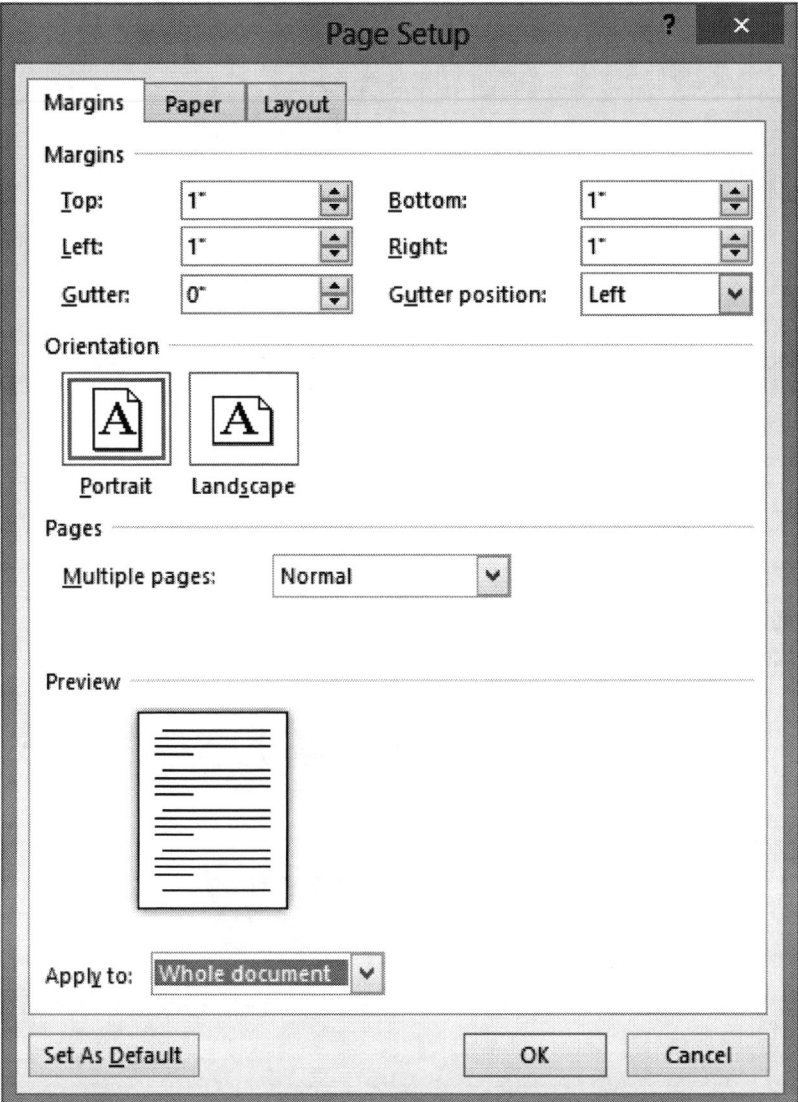

*Figure 7-5: Normal margins set in the Page Setup dialog box.*

Predefined margin types in Word make it easy to set the correct margin for your document.

| Margin Type | Description |
| --- | --- |
| **Normal** | Top, bottom, left, and right margins are at a distance of 1 inch from the page border. |
| **Narrow** | Top, bottom, left, and right margins are at a distance of 0.5 inches from the page border. |
| **Moderate** | Top and bottom margins are at a distance of 1 inch, and left and right margins are at a distance of 0.75 inches from the page border. |
| **Wide** | Top and bottom margins are at a distance of 1 inch, and left and right margins are at a distance of 2 inches from the page border. |
| **Mirrored** | Top and bottom margins are at a distance of 1 inch, inside margins are at a distance of 1.25 inches, and outside margins are at a distance of 1 inch from the page border. |
| **Office 2003 Default** | Top and bottom margins are at a distance of 1 inch, and left and right margins are at a distance of 1.25 inches from the page border. |

### Gutter Margins and Mirrored Margins

Gutter margins add extra space to the left and top margins to accommodate binding or stapling. Mirrored margins are generally used for facing pages, such as those found in a bound document. When you use mirrored margins, the gutter margin is automatically defined.

## Page Orientation

Page orientation refers to the way a page is positioned. The two most common page orientations are portrait and landscape. In portrait orientation, the height of the page is greater than the width. In landscape orientation, the width of the page is greater than its height. Portrait orientation is normally used for books, reports, academic papers, and other formal documents. Landscape orientation is often used for certificates, or for documents containing large tables or graphs. The orientation setting affects the overall layout of text on a page.

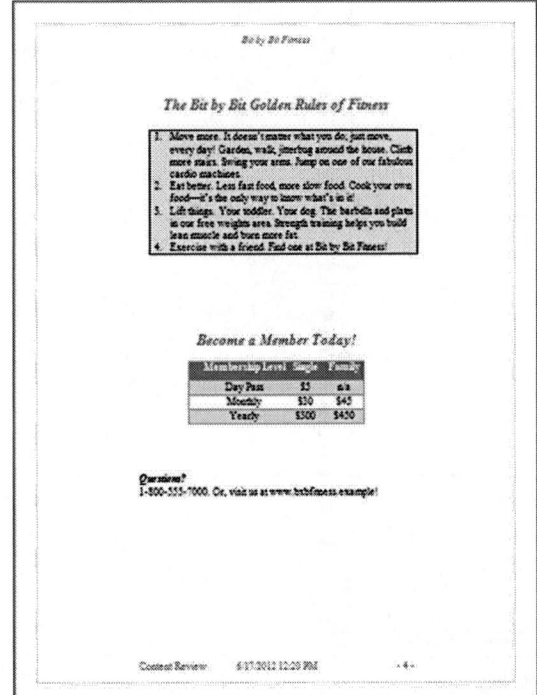
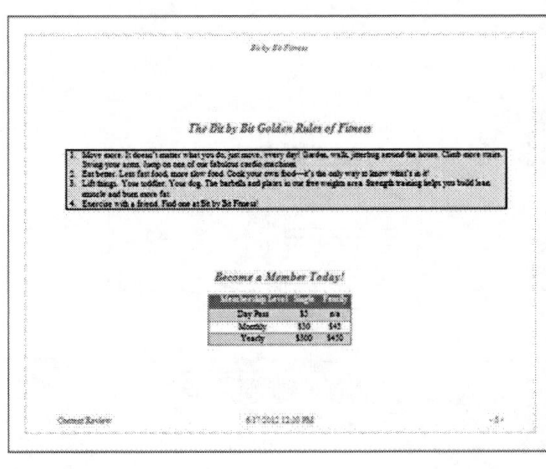

*Figure 7-6: A page in portrait and landscape orientations.*

## Vertical Alignment Options

Just as you can align text horizontally in a document, you can also align it vertically between the top and bottom margins. Vertical alignment options work the same way for both the portrait and landscape page orientations. You can set a vertical alignment option via the **LAYOUT** tab in the **Page Setup** dialog box. This dialog box is accessed from the **Page Setup** dialog box launcher on the **PAGE LAYOUT** tab.

The alignment options help you simplify vertical page layout.

| Alignment Option | Description |
|---|---|
| **Top** | Positions the text along the top margin of a page. This is the Word default setting. |
| **Center** | Positions the text in the center of a page, providing equal amounts of white space above and below the text. |
| **Justified** | Distributes the text equally between the top and bottom margins. |

| Alignment Option | Description |
| --- | --- |
| Bottom | Aligns the text along the bottom margin of a page. |

# The Paper Size Option

Word allows you to adjust your document based on the size of the paper it will be printed on. While the most common paper size in the United States is 8.5" x 11" (the "Letter" size), other paper size options are also available. Changing the paper size also changes the layout of your document, so be sure that whatever size paper you use, you preview the document and adjust your layout before printing. To select the paper size from the **PAGE LAYOUT** tab in the **Page Setup** group, click the **Size** button and select the desired size from the gallery. You can also select a paper size in the **Page Setup** dialog box on the **Paper** tab.

# Page Breaks

A *page break* marks the end of a page of text. You may find, though, that the automatic page breaks that Word inserts don't quite suit how you want your text to flow. Perhaps your document contains a table that would look quite awkward if most of the rows appeared on one page, and one or two appeared on the next. Or, you might want to keep certain paragraphs together on one page, or prevent Word from inserting a break in the middle of a paragraph. In Word, you can insert manual page breaks to keep sections of your document on one page, or to start a new page.

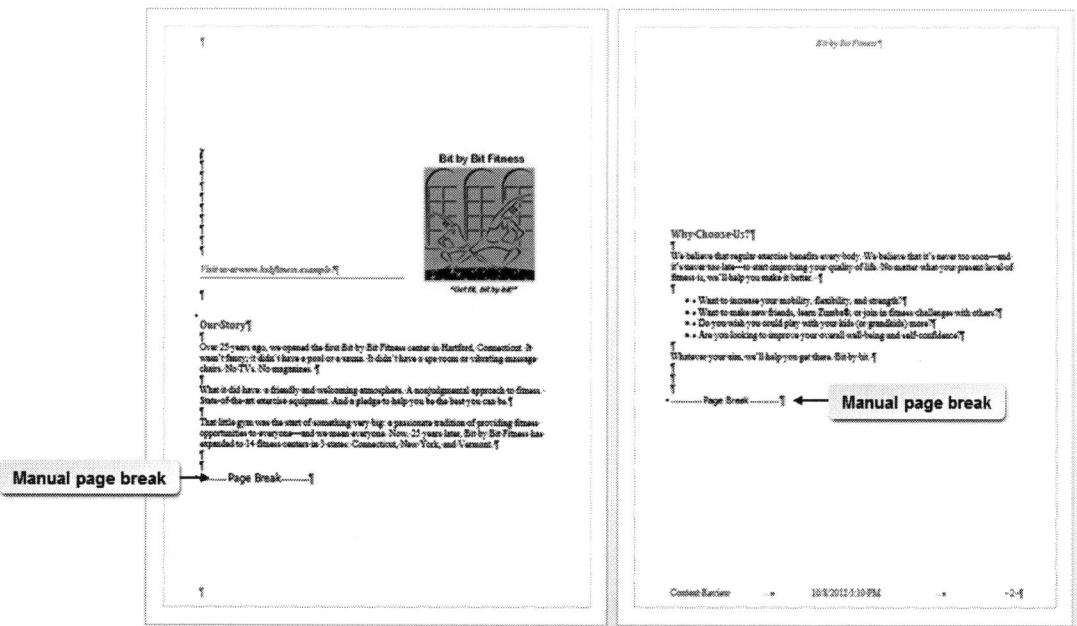

*Figure 7–7: A document with manual page breaks.*

## White Space Between Pages

There is extra white space at the bottom of the page where a break is inserted. This white space can be hidden with the **Show/Hide White Space** feature. It also hides the top and bottom margins of the pages to enable easier scrolling when you are in the **Print Layout** view. When you position the mouse pointer between two pages, the mouse pointer changes to a **Hide White Space** or **Show White Space** pointer. You can toggle between these two modes by double-clicking, or, by pressing **Ctrl** while clicking between the pages.

## The Page Setup Dialog Box

Many of the page layout options you'll frequently use appear on the **PAGE LAYOUT** tab of the ribbon. But you can also set layout options in the **Page Setup** dialog box. There are three tabs in the dialog box: **Margins**, **Paper**, and **Layout**.

| Tab | Description |
| --- | --- |
| **Margins** | Use this tab to set margins and page orientation. Here, you can also specify whether the settings should be applied to the whole document or to specific pages. |
| **Paper** | Use this tab to modify the paper size and paper source for printing. From this tab, you can also access the **Display** tab in the **Word Options** dialog box to customize the display settings of the document. |
| **Layout** | Use this tab to modify sections, headers, and footers; set the vertical alignment of text; and set different styles for the page borders. |

 Access the Checklist tile on your **LogicalCHOICE** course screen for reference information and job aids on **How to Control Page Layout**

# ACTIVITY 7-5
## Controlling Page Layout

### Before You Begin
My Bit by Bit Fitness Draft.docx is open.

### Scenario
You're almost ready to print out your document for the meeting with your coworker to go over the content. Before printing, however, you want to make sure the text and graphics are laid out neatly, and that each section of the document occupies its own page. This will increase the amount of white space in the document to improve the readability of the content, and also to give you and your coworker some space to write notes in.

1. Apply the **Wide** margin setting to the document.
   a) On the **PAGE LAYOUT** tab, in the **Page Setup** group, select **Margins** to open the **Margins** gallery.
   b) From the gallery, select **Wide**.

2. Insert a page break before "Why Choose Us?"
   a) Place the insertion point before "Why Choose Us?"
   b) On the **PAGE LAYOUT** tab, in the **Page Setup** group, select **Breaks**.
   c) From the gallery, select **Page**.

3. Insert a page break before "What We Offer."

4. Set the vertical alignment of the document content to **Center**.
   a) On the **PAGE LAYOUT** tab, in the **Page Setup** group, select the dialog box launcher to open the **Page Setup** dialog box.
   b) In the dialog box, on the **Layout** tab, under **Page**, from the **Vertical alignment** drop-down list, select **Center**.
   c) Under **Preview,** in the **Apply to** box, verify that **Whole document** is selected.

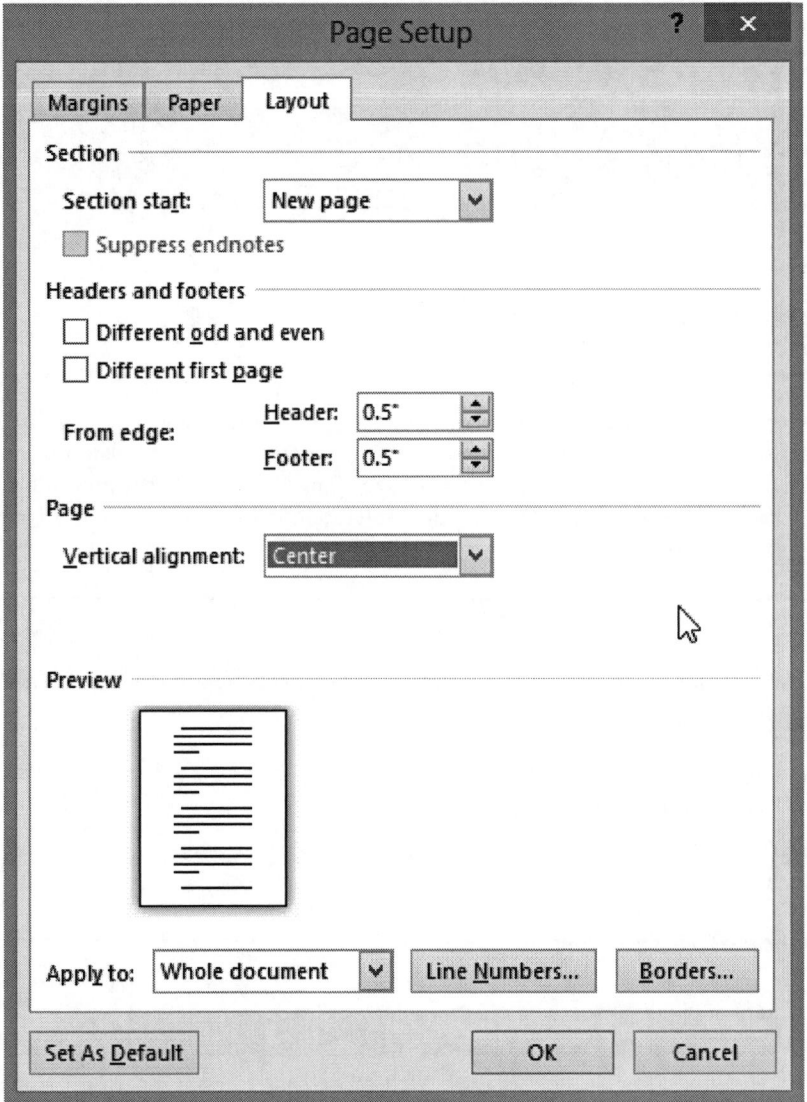

d) Select **OK**.

5. Set the left indent of the first line in the document to 0".

   a) Place the insertion point just before "Visit us at www.bxbfitness.example!"

   b) On the **PAGE LAYOUT** tab, in the **Paragraph** group, in the **Indent Left** spin box, set the value to **0"**.

6. Preview the document.

7. Save your changes, and close the document.

# Summary

In this lesson, you applied various design and layout options to the pages of a document. Adding borders and page colors can give your documents a polished, professional look. Adding elements such as watermarks, headers, and footers are often used to provide useful information about your document. And finally, setting appropriate layout options allow you to configure the margins and page orientation needed for a particular document.

**In what circumstances might you choose, or not choose, to use page elements such as page colors and borders, watermarks, and headers and footers?**

**After learning about page layout options, and thinking about the way you work, are you more likely to set page layout options before entering content into your document, or to wait until you're ready to print? Why?**

> **Note:** Check your LogicalCHOICE Course screen for opportunities to interact with your classmates, peers, and the larger LogicalCHOICE online community about the topics covered in this course or other topics you are interested in. From the Course screen you can also access available resources for a more continuous learning experience.

# 8 | Proofing a Document

**Lesson Time: 30 minutes**

## Lesson Objectives

In this lesson, you will:

- Check spelling and grammar.
- Use other Word proofing tools.
- Check the accessibility of your documents.

## Lesson Introduction

You've applied design and layout options to pages. Another important task before printing is proofing your document for writing errors. An orderly layout with appealing design elements will mean little if your document contains misspelled words and punctuation mistakes. Finding and fixing such errors will go a long way toward projecting a professional image. Luckily, Word provides several powerful tools for making this otherwise time-consuming task quick and easy.

# TOPIC A

## Check Spelling and Grammar

Before finalizing your document, you will want to ensure that it has no spelling or other writing errors. Rather than reading through the document yourself to find mistakes, Word can save you valuable time by doing the checking for you.

Additionally, you might want to know the number of words in your document. Some documents are expected to be a particular length. You might be writing a magazine article, or a business proposal, and the publication or company won't allow you to go over a certain word limit. Before electronic word-processing, most people used a simple formula to calculate an estimated word count. However, Word's word-counting feature is effortless and accurate.

### Spelling and Grammar Check Options

Word provides you with the capability to check the spelling and grammar usage in a document against a built-in dictionary and set of grammar rules. To check the text, on the **REVIEW** tab, in the **Proofing** group, select the **Spelling & Grammar** button. If no spelling or grammar errors are detected, a message indicates this. If a spelling error is found, the **Spelling** pane opens for you to fix the problem or add the word to the dictionary. If a grammar error is found, the **Grammar** pane opens for you to fix the problem. You can also right-click individual suspected errors, and select the desired correction from the shortcut menu. The correction pane can also be accessed from the status bar.

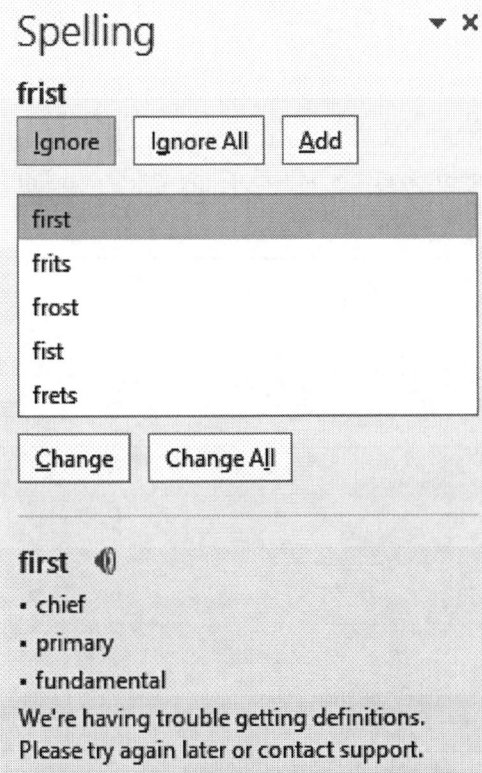

*Figure 8–1: The Spelling pane.*

The **Spelling** pane shows a list of possible words to replace the misspelled word. It also contains several buttons that assist you in reviewing and correcting errors.

| Option | Description |
|---|---|
| Ignore | This button instructs Word to skip the occurrence of the error this time, but find the next occurrence. In this way, you can correct errors on a case-by-case basis. |
| Ignore All | Instructs Word to ignore all instances of the highlighted error, and continue searching for the next error. |
| Add | Instructs Word to add the occurrence of the word or phrase to the dictionary. This will allow Word to recognize the occurrence as correct when you check spelling in the future. |
| Change | Replaces the found text with the selected correction from the **Suggestions** list box. |
| Change All | Replaces all occurrences of the found text with the selected correction from the **Suggestions** list box. |

> **Note:** To further learn about customizing the spelling and grammar checkers, you can access the LearnTO **Customize the Spelling and Grammar Checker** presentation from the **LearnTO** tile on the LogicalCHOICE Course screen.

The **Grammar** pane shows suggestions for how to fix any grammatical errors that are found in the document. You can ignore the error or make the suggested change.

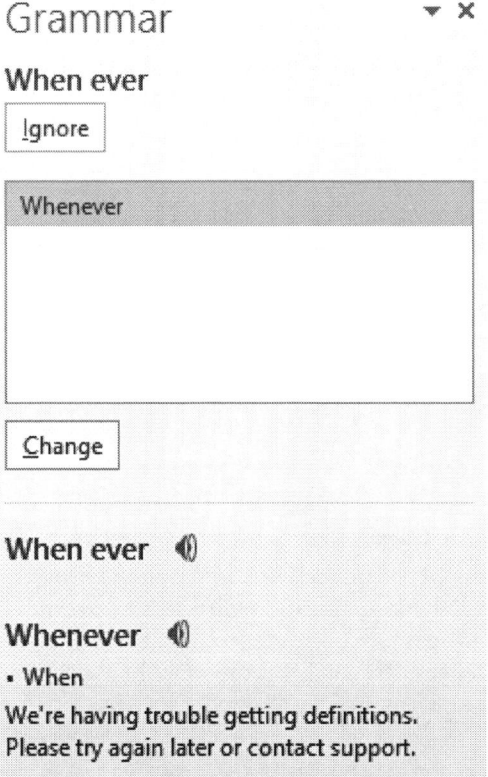

*Figure 8-2: The Grammar pane.*

The grammar rules that are checked are controlled by settings in the **Word Options** in the **Proofing** section. You should review the current settings to make sure that the settings meet your needs. For example, your organization might require two spaces between sentences or might require only one space.

# The Dictionary

When you type, or when you run the **Spelling & Grammar** command, Word compares the words in your document to its internal dictionary. If you have misspelled a word, or if you have used a specialized word that is not in the dictionary, the spell checker will give you a list of possible suggestions. The main dictionary is the primary dictionary used to check for errors. The main dictionary can be neither edited nor viewed. Word also has a default custom dictionary to which you can add words or names.

You can also view the definition of a word. Select a word and then on the **REVIEW** tab, in the **Proofing** group, select **Define**. The **Dictionary** pane opens and shows you the definition for the word.

## Custom Dictionaries

You can also create or import custom dictionaries and remove custom dictionaries when you no longer need them. To manage custom dictionaries, open the **Word Options** dialog box, select the **Proofing** tab, and then select **Custom Dictionaries**.

## Definitions

There is also a dictionary for looking up definitions. It includes a pronunciation feature. Click the speaker icon to hear the word spoken.

### Look Up a Word Definition

To look up the definition of a word:

1. In the document, select the word for which you want to see a definition.
2. On the **REVIEW** tab, in the **Proofing** group, select **Define**. The **Dictionary** pane is displayed.
3. After reviewing the definition, close the **Dictionary** pane.

# The Readability Statistics Dialog Box

Readability statistics are ratings that provide numeric data on the readability of your text. If you have enabled readability statistics in Word, the **Readability Statistics** dialog box is displayed after you check the grammar usage. This dialog box provides detailed information on the total number of characters, words, sentences, and paragraphs in a document; and also the average number of words per sentence, sentences per paragraph, and characters per word in the document. It also reports the readability scores for the content in the document. You enable readability statistics via the **Word Options** dialog box.

## Readability Scores

Word's readability scores are based on the Flesch Reading Ease and the Flesch-Kincaid Grade Level scales. These scales evaluate the readability and complexity of the document based on the average number of syllables per word and words per sentence. A low Flesch Reading Ease score correlates to a high grade level, while a low Flesch-Kincaid Grade Level score correlates to high reading ease level. You can lower the grade level by using simple sentences. Readability scores should match your target audience.

 **Access the Checklist tile on your LogicalCHOICE course screen for reference information and job aids on How to Enable Readability Statistics**

# ACTIVITY 8-1
## Enabling Readability Statistics

### Data Files

C:\091024Data\Proofing a Document\Bit by Bit Fitness Draft.docx

### Scenario

You're concerned about all the documents you produce rating well on readability. You want to ensure that you get a readability score whenever you run a spelling and grammar check, so that you can make adjustments, as necessary. In this activity, you'll enable the display of readability statistics.

1. From the **C:\091024Data\Proofing a Document** folder, open **Bit by Bit Fitness Draft.docx**, and save it as *My Bit by Bit Fitness Draft.docx*

2. Enable the display of readability statistics after a spelling and grammar check.
   a) Select **FILE→Options** to open the **Word Options** dialog box.
   b) In the dialog box, select the **Proofing** tab.
   c) Under **When correcting spelling and grammar in Word**, check **Show readability statistics**.
   d) Select **OK**.

## The Word Count Dialog Box

The **Readability Statistics** dialog box also displays the word count after a spelling and grammar check. However, you can also track the word count as you work on your document. This is important if your document must conform to certain length limits. When you select **WORDS** on the status bar, or when you select the **Word Count** button on the **REVIEW** tab, in the **Proofing** group, the **Word Count** dialog box displays. This dialog box helps you keep track of the number of pages, words, characters, paragraphs, and lines in a document. As you enter text in a document, Word displays a live word count on the status bar.

 **Note:** If you have text selected when you perform a word count, the word count is only for the selected text.

 Access the Checklist tile on your LogicalCHOICE course screen for reference information and job aids on **How to Check the Number of Words in a Document**

 Access the Checklist tile on your LogicalCHOICE course screen for reference information and job aids on **How to Check Spelling and Grammar in a Document**

# ACTIVITY 8-2
## Checking Spelling, Grammar, and Length of a Document

### Before You Begin

My Bit by Bit Fitness Draft.docx is open.

### Scenario

Before you meet with your coworker to go over the content in your draft document, you want to be sure that you haven't made any spelling or grammar errors. You also want to make sure that there are no sentence fragments in the document, that there is agreement between subjects and verbs, and that there is only one space between sentences. You also want to know the number of words and paragraphs in the document. You decide to check for errors and length before printing the document for your meeting.

1. Configure the spelling options.
   a) Select **FILE→Options**.
   b) Select the **Proofing** tab.
   c) Select **Custom Dictionaries**.
   d) Verify that the **RoamingCustom** and **CUSTOM** dictionaries are checked.
   e) Select **OK**.

2. Configure the grammar options.
   a) In the **When correcting spelling and grammar in Word** section, from the **Writing Style** list, select **Grammar & Style**.
   b) Select **Settings**.
   c) From the **Spaces required between sentences** list, select **1**.
   d) Check the **Fragments and Run-ons** check box.
   e) Check the **Subject-verb agreement** check box.
   f) Select **OK** in the dialog boxes to apply the settings and close the dialog boxes.

3. Begin the spelling and grammar check of the entire document.
   a) If the insertion point is not at the top of the document, place it on the first line of the document.
   b) On the **REVIEW** tab, in the **Proofing** group, select **Spelling & Grammar** to start the check.
   c) At the first compound word detection, select **Ignore** to ignore the compound word suggestion. Ignore any additional compound words the grammar checker finds as you continue through the document.
   d) Ignore all of the grammar issues until the **Number Agreement** error is detected.
   e) At the **Number Agreement** error detection, select "a pledge" and select **Change**.
   f) Keep ignoring errors until the spelling error for "Zumba" is detected, and then select **Add**.
   g) Add the word "Cybex" to the dictionary when it is detected.
   h) Ignore the rest of the errors in the grammar check for the document.

4. When you have completed the spelling and grammar check changes, observe the statistics for the document.
   a) The Readability Statistics dialog box opens automatically. Observe the counts for words, characters, paragraphs, and sentences.

      Your numbers might vary compared to those shown in this graphic.

**Readability Statistics**  ?  ×

**Counts**
| | |
|---|---|
| Words | 565 |
| Characters | 2766 |
| Paragraphs | 41 |
| Sentences | 53 |

**Averages**
| | |
|---|---|
| Sentences per Paragraph | 2.2 |
| Words per Sentence | 9.9 |
| Characters per Word | 4.7 |

**Readability**
| | |
|---|---|
| Passive Sentences | 0% |
| Flesch Reading Ease | 66.4 |
| Flesch-Kincaid Grade Level | 6.3 |

OK

b) Observe the averages.
c) Observe the readability statistics.
d) Select **OK**.

5. Save your changes.

# TOPIC B

## Other Proofing Tools

In addition to checking spelling and grammar, Word provides other useful tools to help improve the content of your document. Just as you can use the built-in spell checker in Word to fix writing errors, you can also use a built-in thesaurus to find synonyms for specific words. Sometimes it's difficult to think of appropriate alternatives to a certain word. The thesaurus can help by supplying you with a list of synonyms to choose from.

Additionally, Word provides several other resources for finding information. You can search a foreign-language dictionary or thesaurus, if needed. You can even save valuable time by using one of Word's Internet research sites, without having to leave the Word application.

## The Thesaurus

A *thesaurus* is a reference tool containing a collection of synonyms and antonyms. Unlike a dictionary, a thesaurus does not provide the definition of a word. An electronic thesaurus can suggest and replace words automatically in a document. You can access the Word thesaurus on the **REVIEW** tab, in the **Proofing** group. The thesaurus is also available in **French (France)** and **Spanish (International Sort)**.

 Access the Checklist tile on your LogicalCHOICE course screen for reference information and job aids on How to Use the Thesaurus

# ACTIVITY 8-3
## Using the Thesaurus

### Before You Begin
My Bit by Bit Fitness Draft.docx is open.

### Scenario
In preparing for your meeting with your coworker to go over the content in your document, you noticed a couple of words that you think could be replaced with better alternatives. You decide to let Word suggest alternatives for the words using the thesaurus.

1. Select a synonym for "sociable."
   a) On the first page of the document, in the second paragraph under **Our Story**, right-click the word "sociable" to open a shortcut menu.
   b) In the menu, point to **Synonyms** to display a list of suggested synonyms.
   c) From the list, select **friendly**.

2. In the first item of the bulleted list on page 2, replace the word "improve" with the synonym **increase**.

3. If necessary, select **Ignore Once**.

4. Save your changes.

## The Translation Feature

Using the translation feature in Word, you can select text in the document and have it translated into any of several foreign languages. Word uses built-in bilingual dictionaries, as well as online bilingual dictionaries and online machine translation services. You can look up a translation directly in the **Research** task pane, or use a shortcut menu to open the task pane and translate the text.

You can translate single words, phrases, or entire documents. For entire documents, the file is uploaded to a service where it is translated and sent back to you in the foreign language.

### Use Other Languages

In addition to being able to translate the content of your documents to other languages, you can change the language that you use to edit, display ScreenTips, and find Help. The languages you can use depend on whether you have installed language packs on your computer. If the language you want is not available on your computer, you need to acquire and install the appropriate language pack or language interface pack.

## The Research Task Pane

In addition to translations, the **Research** task pane lets you look up information online. This task pane provides access to several Internet search engines. To use the research options, you need an active Internet connection. To open the **Research** task pane from the **REVIEW** tab, in the **Language** group, select **Translate**.

# The Research Options Dialog Box

The **Research Options** dialog box allows you to add and customize the research sites that you want to access. To open the dialog box select **Research Options** in the **Research** task pane.

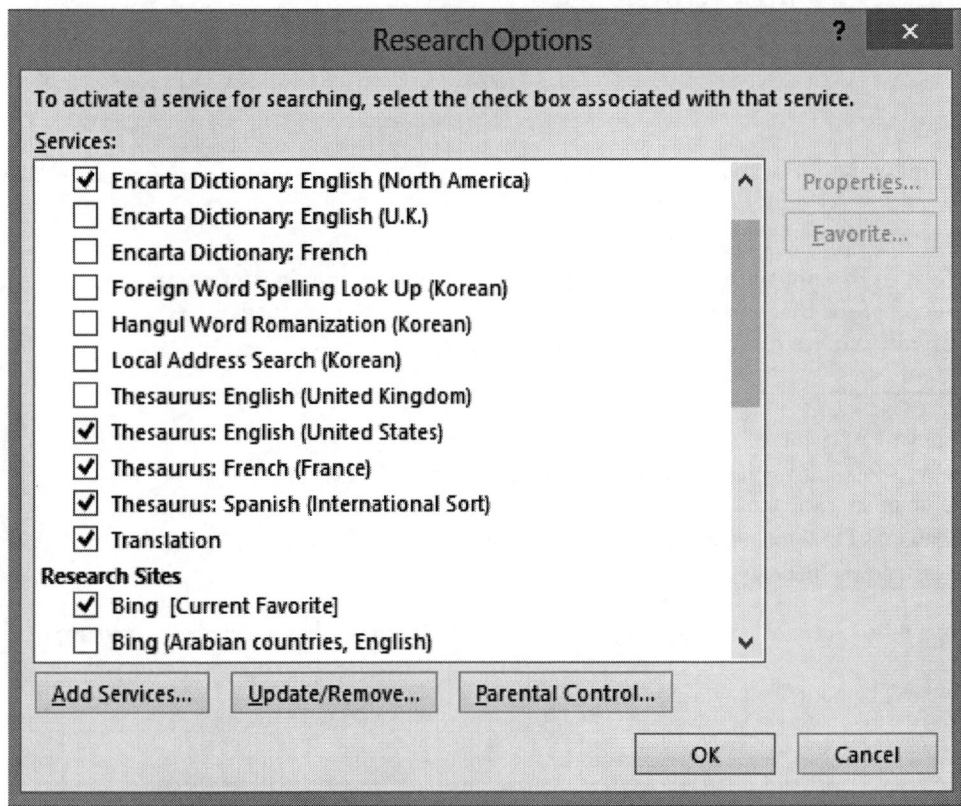

*Figure 8–3: The Research Options dialog box.*

The dialog box contains several options for tailoring research services to your particular needs.

| Option | Description |
|---|---|
| Services | This list contains the current research services available. You can check or uncheck services to include or exclude them from the list of services you use to search for information. |
| Add Services | This button opens the **Add Services** dialog box, where you can specify a web address of the service provider you want to add to your available services list. You can also select the desired service from the **Advertised Services** list box. The list of advertised resources is provided by Microsoft's discovery service. Once you add the desired service, it is displayed in the **Services** list box. |
| Update/ Remove | This button opens the **Update or Remove Services** dialog box, which enables you to update or remove unneeded resources from the **Services** list box. |
| Parental Control | This button opens the **Parental Control** dialog box, where you can restrict the search options in the **Research** task pane. Protecting the research options by setting a password in the **Parental Control** dialog box prevents unauthorized users from accessing the research services. You must be running Word as an administrator to make changes to this feature. |
| Properties | This button opens the **Service Properties** dialog box that contains information about the name of the reference book, its description, copyright details, and the |

| Option | Description |
|---|---|
| | name of its provider. The **Properties** button is active only after a particular reference book is selected from the **Services** list box. |
| Favorite | This button allows you to designate a search service as a favored service. |

 Access the Checklist tile on your LogicalCHOICE course screen for reference information and job aids on **How to Use the Research Task Pane**

# ACTIVITY 8-4

## Using the Research Task Pane

### Before You Begin

My Bit by Bit Fitness Draft.docx is open.

### Scenario

As you review your document, you decide that you would like to translate some of the text into another language. Additionally, you'd like to learn more about Cybex, one of the equipment brands used in Bit by Bit Fitness centers, in case you are ever asked about it by a member. In this activity, you'll use the **Research** task pane to find information.

1. Translate "Our Story" to other languages.
   a) Select the text "Our Story" near the top of the document.
   b) On the **REVIEW** tab, in the **Language** group, select **Translate→Translate Selected Text**.
   c) In the **Research** pane, under **Translation** from the **To** list, select the language of your choice.
      Each word is shown with the foreign word and a definition.
   d) Translate the text to another language of your choice.

2. Find information on the web for the equipment company Cybex.
   a) In the **Search for** text box, delete "Our Story" and type *Cybex*
   b) Under the text box, the resource list is currently set to **Translation**. Select the resource list drop-down arrow to open the list.
   c) From the list, under **All Research Sites**, select **Bing**.

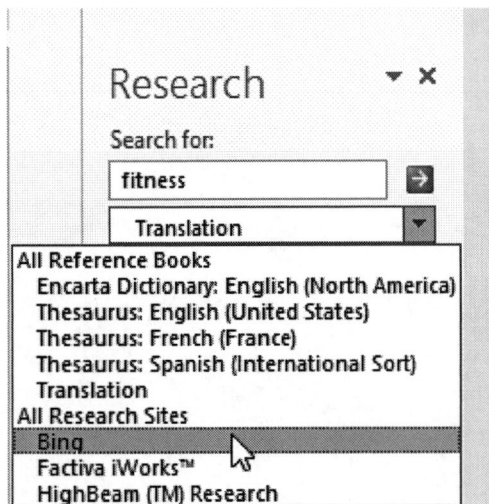

   d) In the search results, select the web address for the Cybex International Exercise Equipment company to open the company's website in a browser window.
   e) Close the browser window and the **Research** task pane.

3. If necessary, save any changes.

# TOPIC C

## Check Accessibility

After you've created your Word document, you may want to check the accessibility of your Word documents.

## Accessibility

People with visual and cognitive disabilities can use supplemental applications to read content that is usually displayed on a computer screen. Documents can be confusing to the reader application if the layout doesn't meet the standard layout the reader expects. Also, readers don't know how to handle images, charts, and some tables. Using attributes on those document components, you can add alternative text the reader reads to the user to give them a sense of what the image or chart shows.

### Alternative Text

Alternative text is displayed when the user positions the mouse pointer over an image or other object in a Word document. For individuals using screen readers, the alternative text is read so that the user hears a description for the image or object. Alternative text is also known as Alt Text. It can be defined as a property of any of these objects in a document:

- Images including pictures and clip art.
- Charts.
- Tables.
- Shapes that are not included in a group and that do not contain text.
- SmartArt graphics.
- Embedded objects.
- Links.
- Video and audio files.
- Grouped objects.

### Table Accessibility

There are several things you can do to make tables more accessible to individuals using screen readers.

- Make sure that tables have column headings that clearly indicate what is contained in the table.
- Avoid nesting tables.
- Avoid merging and splitting cells in tables.
- Avoid unnecessary blank cells which the screen reader might interpret as the end of the table.
- Structure tables so that they are read from left to right and top to bottom.

### Styles

Using paragraph and heading styles can help individuals using screen readers to understand how your document flows. The heading styles can also be used to create a Table of Contents which is also helpful. Content in Heading style paragraphs should be short. Try to keep headings to a single line, usually under 20 words.

When you apply Heading styles, be sure that they are applied in descending order. Start with a Heading 1 style. If you have content that should fall at a lower level within that section of the document, apply Heading 2 (not 3 or 4). If you then have content that should fall at a lower level within Heading 2, apply Heading 3 and so on. This will help users when they are navigating through the document.

### Hyperlink ScreenTips

If you include a hyperlink to content on a web page or other location, be sure to add a ScreenTip so that when the user points to the link text, the ScreenTip is displayed. Be sure that the text provides a good description of the link destination and not just the URL of the link.

### Blank Characters

Avoid using multiple spaces, tabs, or empty paragraphs to format your document. Screen readers interpret these as blank and users might think they are at the end of the document. Use appropriate formatting to create the desired white space.

### Floating Objects

If you have images in your document, they should use the text wrapping option **In line with text** or **Top and Bottom**. Other text wrapping styles make it difficult for screen readers to correctly navigate through the document.

### Watermarks

Watermark images might be difficult for screen readers to interpret properly. Also, individuals with visual and cognitive disabilities often have a hard time understanding the watermark. If watermarks are used, you should also include the information somewhere else in your document, such as in a footer.

### Closed Captions

If your document includes audio, be sure that the audio is included in another format. Typically you will use closed captioning, but you can also use transcripts or alt text.

# Section 508

Section 508 is part of the United States Rehabilitation Act of 1973. It requires all federal agencies to provide access to information so that any person can access it whether they are disabled or not. Section 508 includes technical standards documents that must be adhered to so that 508 compliance can be achieved.

 **Note:** If you need more information about Section 508 compliance, refer to **http://www.section508.gov**.

# Accessibility Checker

A new feature in the Office 2013 products is the Accessibility Checker. This tool checks documents for anything in your document that would be a challenge for a disabled user to access.

The Accessibility Checker flags issues as either an error, a warning, or a tip. Errors indicate that the content in the file would be difficult or impossible for a disabled person to understand. Items flagged as warnings would be difficult for most disabled persons to understand. Items flagged as tips can most likely be understood by a disabled person, but you might be able to present it in a better way or organize the information in a different way to make it more understandable by disabled persons.

### Errors

Items in the following table will be flagged as errors by the Accessibility Checker.

| Rule | Items Checked |
| --- | --- |
| All objects have alternate text | Checks that objects in the document have alternate text defined and that the alternate text does not contain any images or file extensions. |

| Rule | Items Checked |
|------|---------------|
| Tables specify column header information | Checks that tables use the Table Normal style or have a header row defined. |
| Long documents use styles to provide structure | Checks that heading styles are used to organize the content. It also checks whether a Table of Contents has been included. One or the other, or both, are required to meet accessibility standards. |

## Warnings

Items in the following table will be flagged as warnings by the Accessibility Checker.

| Rule | Items Checked |
|------|---------------|
| Hyperlink text is meaningful | Checks that link text in a hyperlink has a ScreenTip and that it matches the link target. |
| Table has simple structure | Checks that tables do not contain split cells, merged cells, or nested tables. Any table that is not rectangular will cause the table to be flagged with a warning. |
| Tables don't use blank cells for formatting | Checks that there are no blank columns or rows in tables. |
| Avoid the use of repeated 'blank' characters | Checks that multiple blank spaces, tabs, or paragraphs are included in the document. |
| Headings don't contain too much information | Checks that headings are not too long. |
| The use of floating objects is avoided | Checks that objects with text wrapping are configured as in line with text. |

## Tips

Items in the following table will be flagged as tips by the Accessibility Checker.

| Rule | Items Checked |
|------|---------------|
| Closed captions are included for inserted audio and video | Checks that audio objects and video objects have been configured to use closed captioning. |
| Layout Tables are structured for easy navigation | Checks that the order of cells is logical for the language being used and that the tab order is not circular. This means that languages which are read left to right should have tables that read from left to right. |
| No image watermarks are used | Checks that watermarks are not used in the document. |
| All headings are in the correct order | Checks that the Heading styles have been applied in order starting with Heading 1, followed by Heading 2, Heading 3, and so forth. |

 **Access the Checklist tile on your LogicalCHOICE course screen for reference information and job aids on How to Create Accessible Word Documents**

# ACTIVITY 8-5
## Checking Accessibility

### Before You Begin
My Bit by Bit Fitness Draft.docx is open.

### Scenario
You have checked the spelling and grammar on your document. You want to make sure the document will be accessible to anyone who will be using a screen reader.

1. Check the accessibility of your document.
   a) Select **FILE→Info**.
   b) Select **Check for Issues→Check Accessibility**.
      The **Accessibility Checker** task pane opens and lists any **ERRORS**, **WARNINGS**, or **TIPS** found in the document.
   c) Select an issue to display additional information including why you should fix the issue and how to fix the issue.

2. Fix any errors displayed in the **Inspection Results**.

3. If necessary, save any changes and close the file.

# Summary

In this lesson, you used several proofing tools to not only make your documents more accurate, but also to find information about some of the words in your document. These tools can assist you with the mechanics of review and revision so that you can produce clear and interesting documents.

**Which proofing tools do you think you'll use most frequently?**

**How do you think the proofing tools will help you in creating professional documents?**

 **Note:** Check your LogicalCHOICE Course screen for opportunities to interact with your classmates, peers, and the larger LogicalCHOICE online community about the topics covered in this course or other topics you are interested in. From the Course screen you can also access available resources for a more continuous learning experience.

# 9 | Customizing the Word Environment

**Lesson Time: 45 minutes**

## Lesson Objectives

In this lesson, you will:

- Customize the Word interface.

- Use additional Save options.

## Lesson Introduction

The more you work with Word and become familiar with its many features and tools, the faster you will be able to produce professional documents. If you're like many people, you appreciate knowing shortcuts for repetitive tasks. Having to click several buttons to accomplish a routine task can be a nuisance when you want to focus on your writing.

At times, you'll probably need to adjust the way Word saves a particular document. Perhaps you're sending a document to someone who doesn't have Microsoft® Word 2013 installed, so they will need to use another application in order to read it. Or, you might want to make sure Word is configured to save your documents at regular intervals, so you don't risk losing all your hard work should your computer crash. Fortunately, Word offers many choices for optimizing the user environment that suit the way you work.

# TOPIC A

## Customize the Word Interface

Now that you've become more comfortable with the user interface, you may find yourself wondering if there are ways to make your work flow faster. You might wish for an alternative to constantly typing out a long name that you use regularly, or clicking in several places simply to open a document. Word's default interface may not suit the way you typically work. Luckily, you can change the interface to streamline the tasks you perform frequently.

### The Word Options Dialog Box

The **Word Options** dialog box contains various commands that help you customize the Word environment to suit your particular needs. Select **FILE→Options** to open this dialog box. Each tab in the **Word Options** dialog box contains commands associated with a particular category of tasks.

| Tab | Contains Commands To |
| --- | --- |
| General | Personalize the work environment by setting the color scheme, user name, and start-up options. It also allows you to enable or disable the **Mini** toolbar and **Live Preview** features. |
| Display | Modify how text content is displayed on screen and when printed. You can opt to show or hide certain page elements such as highlighter and formatting marks. |
| Proofing | Specify how Word should correct and format text that you type. You can set the auto-correction settings and ensure that Word corrects all spelling and grammatical errors. You can also ensure that Word ignores certain words or errors in a document, and turn off **AutoCorrect**. |
| Save | Specify the customization options for saving documents. Depending on how often you want to save the backup information of your documents, you can specify the frequency at which a document will be auto-saved. You can also change the default location of where documents will be saved. |
| Language | Modify the Word language preferences. |
| Advanced | Specify options for editing, copying, pasting, displaying, printing, saving, and writing content. It also provides advanced options needed to work with Word. |
| Customize Ribbon | Customize the ribbon. Using the options on this tab, you can select the additional tabs, groups, and commands that you want to display on the ribbon. |
| Quick Access Toolbar | Customize the **Quick Access Toolbar**. Using the options on this tab, you can select the commands that you want to add to the **Quick Access Toolbar**. You can also opt to position the **Quick Access Toolbar** below the ribbon. |
| Add-Ins | Manage any extensions you are using to enhance Office applications. Extensions are add-ins that introduce new functionality to an application. Many add-ins are installed with Office 2013. |
| Trust Center | Secure the system and documents. Using the **Advanced Trust Center Settings** button on this tab, you can set the security measures that are needed to secure a document. |

**Note:** To further learn about customizing Word, you can access the LearnTO **Apply Other Word Customizations** presentation from the **LearnTO** tile on the LogicalCHOICE Course screen.

 **Access the Checklist tile on your LogicalCHOICE course screen for reference information and job aids on How to Customize the Quick Access Toolbar**

# ACTIVITY 9–1
## Customizing the Quick Access Toolbar

### Before You Begin
Make sure Word is open.

### Scenario
You've been working with Word for a while now, but some simple tasks seem to take longer to perform than you'd like. You are constantly creating new documents and opening existing documents, and frequently formatting your text. You decide to add some commands to the **Quick Access Toolbar** to save time when you carry out these tasks.

---

1. Open the **Word Options** dialog box, and select the **Quick Access Toolbar** tab.

   a) Select **FILE→Options**.
   b) Select the **Quick Access Toolbar** tab.

2. Add the **New** command to the toolbar.

   a) In the **Commands** list, scroll down and select **New**.

   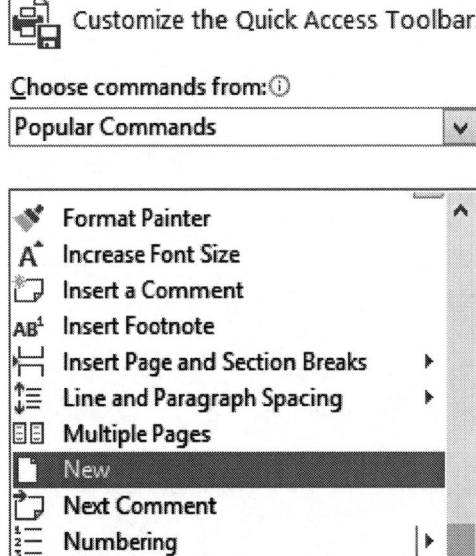

   b) Select **Add** to add the **New** command to the toolbar.

3. Add the **Open** command to the toolbar.

4. Add the **Close** command to the toolbar.

   a) In the **Choose commands from** list, select **File Tab** to open a list of commands available on the FILE tab.

Customize the Quick Access Toolbar.

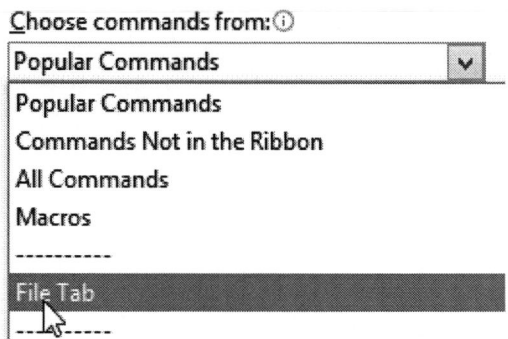

b) From the list of available commands, select the **Close** command and select **Add**.

5. Select **OK** to close the **Word Options** dialog box.

6. Add the **HOME** tab **Paragraph** group to the **Quick Access Toolbar**.

   a) On the **HOME** tab, right-click the **Paragraph** group, and choose **Add to Quick Access Toolbar**.

7. Verify that the **Quick Access Toolbar** displays the added commands.

 **Access the Checklist tile on your LogicalCHOICE course screen for reference information and job aids on How to Customize the Ribbon**

# ACTIVITY 9-2
## Customizing the Ribbon

### Before You Begin
Word is already open.

### Scenario
As you look for ways to increase your efficiency, you notice that there are commands from different tab groups that you use quite a bit. It would help to have these commands grouped together in one location so that you don't have to keep switching between tabs to access them. You decide to collect these frequently used commands into a new group on a new tab.

 **Note:** As you perform this activity, note that you can add commands to tab groups only, not to tabs themselves.

1. Create a new tab on the ribbon.
   a) Open the **Word Options** dialog box, and select the **Customize Ribbon** tab.
   b) Under the right pane, select **New Tab** to create a new tab after the **HOME** tab.

2. Rename the new tab and new group.
   a) In the right pane, select **New Tab (Custom)**.
   b) Select **Rename**.

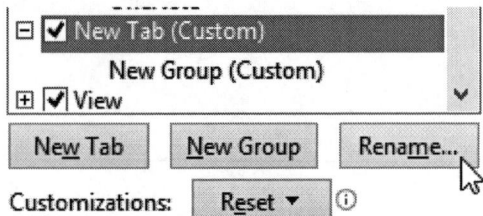

   c) Type *MY FAVORITES* and select **OK**.
   d) Rename **New Group (Custom)** as **Favorites**.

3. Add commands to the **Favorites** group.
   a) In the **Commands** list, select **Align Left**, and select **Add**.
   b) Add the following commands: **Center**, **Print Preview and Print**, and **Spelling & Grammar**.

4. Move the **MY FAVORITES** tab to the end.
   a) Select **MY FAVORITES (Custom)** from the right pane.
   b) Select the down arrow on the right until it is grayed out.
   c) Select **OK**.

5. Select the **MY FAVORITES** tab, and verify that the new commands appear in the **Favorites** group.

# The AutoCorrect Dialog Box

You can use the **AutoCorrect** dialog box to control how Word automatically corrects errors. Open the **AutoCorrect** dialog box by selecting **FILE→Options**, and in the **Word Options** dialog box, select the **Proofing** tab, and then select **AutoCorrect Options**.

The **AutoCorrect** dialog box contains several tabs to help you configure **AutoCorrect** behavior.

| Tab | Options |
| --- | --- |
| **AutoCorrect** | Automatically edit typographical or capitalization errors. |
| **Math AutoCorrect** | Automatically replace expressions with the corresponding symbols. |
| **AutoFormat As You Type** | Automatically format the document text as you type. |
| **AutoFormat** | Automatically format certain elements of a document. |
| **Actions** | Perform additional actions for some words and phrases via the right-click menu. |

# The AutoCorrect Tab

The **AutoCorrect** tab in the **AutoCorrect** dialog box contains a number of options that instruct Word to fix certain errors. You can enable or disable any of these options, and you can add and delete exceptions to certain options.

The AutoCorrect options are described in the following table.

| Option | Instructs Word To |
| --- | --- |
| **Show AutoCorrect Options buttons** | Display the **AutoCorrect Options** button whenever the **AutoCorrect** feature edits a typographical error. |
| **Correct TWo INitial CApitals** | Correct the error of typing two initial capitals for a word. |
| **Capitalize first letter of sentences** | Capitalize the initial letter of every sentence. |
| **Capitalize first letter of table cells** | Capitalize the initial letter of words in each cell of a table. |
| **Capitalize names of days** | Capitalize the initial letters of day names. |
| **Correct accidental usage of cAPS LOCK key** | Correct the casing of the letters in a sentence, if **Caps Lock** is accidentally activated. |
| **Exceptions** | Open a dialog box where you can type exceptions to the **AutoCorrect** options selected. You can also delete exceptions here. |
| **Replace text as you type** | Replace common typographical errors or other key combinations with designated words or characters. For example, as a shortcut for the words that you frequently type, such as your company's name, you can enter an abbreviation that Word will expand to the full word or phrase. You should not add words that already exist in the list as shortcuts for other words. |

 Access the Checklist tile on your LogicalCHOICE course screen for reference information and job aids on How to Set AutoCorrect Options

# ACTIVITY 9-3
## Setting AutoCorrect Options

### Data Files

C:\091024Data\Customizing the Word Environment\Bit by Bit Fitness Draft.docx

### Scenario

You type your company's name, Bit by Bit Fitness, quite frequently. It would save some time if you had a shortcut that would automatically type out the name for you. You decide to create this shortcut in **AutoCorrect**.

---

1. From the **C:\091024Data\Customizing the Word Environment** folder, open **Bit by Bit Fitness Draft.docx**, and then save it to the current folder as *My Bit by Bit Fitness Draft.docx*

2. Create a shortcut for the text "Bit by Bit Fitness."
   a) Select **FILE→Options** to open the **Word Options** dialog box.
   b) In the **Word Options** dialog box, select the **Proofing** tab.
   c) Select **AutoCorrect Options** to open the **AutoCorrect** dialog box.
   d) Under **Replace text as you type,** in the **Replace** text box, type *bbf*
   e) In the **With** text box, type *Bit by Bit Fitness*
   f) Select **Add**.
   g) Select **OK** to close the **AutoCorrect** dialog box, and then close the **Word Options** dialog box.

3. Verify that your replacement text is functional.
   a) In the document, under **Why Choose Us?**, click at the beginning of the first line.
   b) Type *At bbf,*
   c) Press the **Spacebar** to replace the text.
   d) Type *we're fanatics about health and fitness.*

4. Save your changes.

---

# TOPIC B

## Additional Save Options

You can save a document in Word simply by choosing **Save** on the **FILE** tab, or clicking the **Save** button on the **Quick Access Toolbar**. But what if you need to send your document to a person who doesn't have Word 2013 installed, or who needs to view the document in another application altogether? Or, suppose you receive a Word document that was created in an earlier version of Word? You might have trouble viewing certain elements of the document when you open it.

Additionally, you want to be sure you don't lose any work in case of a power outage, or some other event that shuts down Word without warning. You can modify certain **Save** options to prevent this type of data loss.

## Word 2013 File Formats

A *file format* refers to the way the information in a file is encoded. Different types of files have different file formats. Word 2013 files are saved in the Open XML (eXtensible Markup Language) file format. The Word XML format is a compact and robust file format that enables easy integration of Word documents with other applications and platforms. Word 2013 also supports a number of other file formats.

Some typical file formats you might use include the following.

| File Format | Description |
| --- | --- |
| **Word Document (.docx)** | The default file format in which Word 2013 documents are saved. |
| **Word Macro-Enabled Document (.docm)** | The basic XML file format that can store Visual Basic for Applications (VBA) macro code. Macros are sets of Word commands and instructions grouped as a single command. VBA helps in modifying these macros. |
| **Word 97–2003 Document (.doc)** | The file format that is used to save documents in the 97–2003 versions of Word. It is also used to save documents in the Word 6.0/95 format. |
| **Word Template (.dotx)** | The default format for a Word template. It is used for saving document styles and formatting. |
| **Word Macro-Enabled Template (.dotm)** | The default format for a Word macro-enabled template. Word 2013 stores macro code for use with other Word documents. By default, documents are saved as .docx files even when created from a Word 2013 XML macro-enabled template. |
| **Word 97–2003 Template (.dot)** | Enables you to save a Word template in the 97–2003 version. |
| **Portable Document Format (.pdf)** | Enables you to save a Word document in the Adobe Portable Document Format (PDF). |
| **Web Page (.htm)** | Allows you to save the document as a web page, using the Hypertext Markup Language (HTML) file format. |

## Advantages of the XML File Format

The default file format of Word versions prior to 2007 was .doc. The XML-based .docx file format provides several improvements to the .doc file format that are useful for end users. The advantages of the .docx file format are described in the following table.

| Feature | Advantage |
|---|---|
| Smaller file size | The XML file formats use file compression to reduce file sizes by as much as 75%. These file formats reduce the disk space that is required to store files, as well as the bandwidth needed to share documents across networks. |
| Improved information recovery | The files saved in these formats are modularly structured. The different data components in a file are stored separately. Therefore, a file can be opened even if a component within the file is damaged or corrupted. |
| Easier detection of documents with macros | The file formats with their distinct extensions make it easier to distinguish files that contain macros from those that do not. File extensions ending with "x" cannot contain VBA macros or ActiveX controls, whereas files ending with "m" can. |
| Easier integration and interoperability of information | Other applications, across various platforms, can easily use information created within the Office applications. |

## PDF Files

In addition to being able to save Word files as PDF files, you can also open and edit PDF files in Word. If the PDF file contains fillable fields or other interactive content, those fields cannot be filled in and drop-down lists are not active while the PDF file is open in Word. You can, however, make changes to the static text in the document and save it as a PDF file. When it is opened again in a PDF Reader application, the fillable fields and interactive content will be accessible.

 **Access the Checklist tile on your LogicalCHOICE course screen for reference information and job aids on How to Save a Word Document in a Different File Format**

# ACTIVITY 9-4

## Saving a Word Document in a Different File Format

### Before You Begin

My Bit by Bit Fitness Draft.docx is open.

### Scenario

You'd like to save the document in a fixed file format, for reading purposes only. This is so no one reviewing the document can make unauthorized revisions. You decide that the best file format for this purpose is the .pdf format.

1. Save **My Bit by Bit Fitness Draft.docx** as a PDF file.
   a) Select **FILE→Save As**.
   b) On the **Save As** screen, make sure that **Computer** is selected.
   c) Under **Computer**, under **Current Folder**, select the current folder, **C:\091024Data\Customizing the Word Environment**.
   d) In the **Save As** dialog box, from the **Save as type** drop-down list, select **PDF**.
   e) To the right of **Optimize for** verify that **Standard (publishing online and printing)** is selected.
   f) Select **Save** to save the PDF file with the existing name.

   Because the file has a different extension than the Word file, it will not overwrite the Word file that has the same name.

2. View the PDF file in the PDF Reader.
   a) If the PDF file does not open automatically, on the taskbar on your **Desktop**, select **File Explorer**.

 **Note:** You can use **Alt+Tab** to switch to the **Desktop** and then select the **File Explorer** icon.

   b) Navigate to **C:\091024Data\Customizing the Word Environment**.
   c) Open the PDF file.

   The PDF file has a red icon. You can double-click the file or right-click and select **Open**.

   d) Scroll through the file.
   e) Close the PDF Reader.

3. Save the .docx file.

4. Open the PDF file in Word and make changes to the file.
   a) In Word, select **FILE→Open→Computer**.
   b) In the **Recent Folders** list, select **Customizing the Word Environment**.
   c) If necessary, select **All Word Documents**.
   d) Select and open the PDF version of **My Bit by Bit Fitness Draft**.

   Notice that the icon to the left of the file name is a red PDF icon rather than the blue Word icon.

   e) Select **OK** to allow Word to convert the PDF into an editable Word document.

f)  On page 3, remove some of the blank lines so that the text on page 4 is moved up onto page 3.

g)  Save the file again as a PDF file.

5.  Verify that the change appears in the PDF reader and then close the reader and the .pdf file in Word.

# Compatibility Checker

The **Compatibility Checker** feature in Word 2013 allows you to check different document formats for compatibility with other versions of Word. Some elements in your document may be disabled in order for users of earlier Word versions to view the document, so it's a good idea to run a check for any compatibility issues before sharing the document. If any issues are found, you can save the document in the file format of the earlier version of Word.

## Compatibility Mode

When you open a document created in an earlier version of Word, you will view it in compatibility mode. Some features of Word 2013 are not available in this mode; this ensures that you won't be able to add anything to the document that isn't supported by earlier versions. To enable these features, you can save the document in the .docx file format.

 **Access the Checklist tile on your LogicalCHOICE course screen for reference information and job aids on How to Use the Compatibility Checker**

# ACTIVITY 9-5
## Using the Compatibility Checker

### Before You Begin
My Bit by Bit Fitness Draft.docx is open.

### Scenario
You may be sharing your document with employees at other Bit by Bit Fitness centers. Because you don't know which version of Word everyone is using, you want to make sure that there are no compatibility issues in your document that could be a problem for those with earlier versions. You decide to run the **Compatibility Checker** to determine whether any issues exist.

1. Run the **Compatibility Checker**.
   a) Select **FILE→Info**.
   b) Select **Check for Issues**, and, from the menu, select **Check Compatibility**.
   c) In the **Microsoft Word Compatibility Checker**, select **Select versions to show**, and if necessary, check all versions in the list.

2. Read the information about the issue found. If your document is viewed in an earlier version of Word, the layout will look different. You may opt to share the PDF version of the document, rather than adjust the layout to clear the compatibility issue.

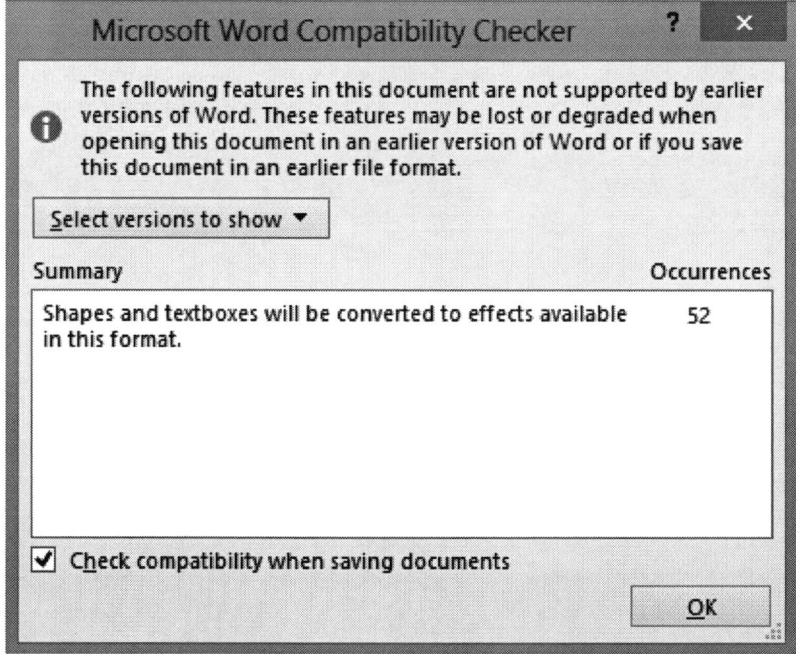

3. Select **OK** to close the **Compatibility Checker**.

## AutoSave

By default, Word automatically saves your documents every 10 minutes, using the **AutoSave** feature. Each time the document is autosaved, a version of the document is created. You can change the **AutoSave** interval in the **Word Options** dialog box. You can also set options to save the document in a specific format, retain the last autosaved version of the document that is closed without saving, and set the location where the file will be saved.

 **Access the Checklist tile on your LogicalCHOICE course screen for reference information and job aids on How to Change AutoSave Options**

# ACTIVITY 9-6
## Changing AutoSave Options

### Before You Begin
My Bit by Bit Fitness Draft.docx is open.

### Scenario
The Bit by Bit Fitness center you work in is in an area that experiences frequent power outages. You'd like to be sure that, in the event the power goes out while you're working on a document, you don't lose too much of your work. You decide to modify the default **AutoSave** interval, so that Word will automatically save your documents a little more frequently.

 **Note:** Be aware that frequent autosaving will use up computer resources, so it's a good idea not to set the interval at too low a value. However, for the purposes of this activity, a low value is necessary to test the **AutoRecover** function later.

Set the **AutoSave** interval to **1** minute.
a) Open the **Word Options** dialog box, and select the **Save** tab.
b) Under **Save documents**, in the **Save AutoRecover information every <value> minutes** spin box, enter *1*
c) Select **OK** in the **Word Options** dialog box.

## AutoRecover

The **AutoRecover** feature of Word 2013 will recover documents that were closed without saving. This can be tremendously helpful should you suffer a power outage, or simply fail to save any changes before closing the document. When you recover an unsaved document, Word opens the last autosaved version of the file.

 **Access the Checklist tile on your LogicalCHOICE course screen for reference information and job aids on How to Recover an Unsaved Document**

## ACTIVITY 9–7

### Recovering an Unsaved Document

### Before You Begin

My Bit by Bit Fitness Draft.docx is open.

### Scenario

You set the **AutoRecover** interval to **AutoSave** your documents more frequently. It's very important that you not lose your data in the event of a power failure or computer malfunction. You'd like to test whether Word is able to recover an unsaved document, so you decide to make a change to your document, then close it without saving it, and try to recover it.

---

1. Make a change to **My Bit by Bit Fitness Draft.docx**, and close it without saving the change.
   a) On the first page of the document, edit "Our Story" to read *Our History*
   b) Wait one minute to allow **AutoSave** to save the document.
   c) Close the document, and select **Don't Save**.

2. Reopen the file from the **Recent** tab.
   a) Select **FILE**.
   b) On the **Open** tab under **Recent Documents**, select the first **My Bit by Bit Fitness Draft** document in the list.
   c) Verify that your recent change was not saved.

3. Recover the unsaved document.
   a) On the **FILE→Info** tab, under **Versions**, select **Today**, *time* **(when I closed without saving)**.

    **Note:** Ensure that the variables listed in the version recovery step match with the most recent **AutoSave**.

   b) At the top of the document area, select **Restore**.
   c) Select **OK** in the message box to allow Word to overwrite the last saved version with the selected version.
   d) Verify that the recent change was restored.

4. Close the document and Word.

---

# Summary

In this lesson, you customized Word to suit the way you work. You also worked with other save options, using Word's powerful tools for saving documents in different file formats, and you recovered unsaved documents. These tools will ensure that you optimize your productivity when using Word, and minimize any possible loss of your work.

**How do you think you might customize the Word interface to suit your individual work habits?**



**In your opinion, what is especially valuable about the additional save options in Word?**

 **Note:** Check your LogicalCHOICE Course screen for opportunities to interact with your classmates, peers, and the larger LogicalCHOICE online community about the topics covered in this course or other topics you are interested in. From the Course screen you can also access available resources for a more continuous learning experience.

# Course Follow-Up

Congratulations on completing the *Microsoft® Office Word 2013: Part 1* course! This course has equipped you with the fundamental skills needed to create, edit, and enhance simple Word 2013 documents. You've learned to navigate around the Word interface; to create new documents and edit them; and how to use the **Word Help** feature for any questions you might have. You've also learned formatting and layout methods for text, paragraphs, and pages. You've gained experience in using Word's powerful tools, including its proofing tools, document recovery features, and customization options. These skills will help you put a professional polish on all of your Word 2013 work.

## What's Next?

Now that you have acquired the basic skills needed to create Word documents, you may want to take your exploration of Word 2013 to the next level with *Microsoft® Office Word 2013: Part 2*. In this Logical Operations course, you'll not only learn some advanced formatting and layout techniques, you'll also learn to speed up professional document creation with such useful tools as **Quick Parts**, templates, and macros.

You are encouraged to explore Word further by actively participating in any of the social media forums set up by your instructor or training administrator through the **Social Media** tile on the LogicalCHOICE Course screen.

# A | Microsoft Office Word 2013 Exam 77-418

Selected Logical Operations courseware addresses Microsoft Office Specialist (MOS) certification skills for Microsoft Office 2013. The following table indicates where Word 2013 skills that are tested on Exam 77-418 are covered in the Logical Operations Microsoft Office Word 2013 series of courses.

| Objective Domain | Covered In |
| --- | --- |
| **1.0 Create and Manage Documents** | |
| **1.1 Create a Document** | |
| 1.1.1 Create new blank documents | Part 1, Topic 1-B |
| 1.1.2 Create new documents using templates | Part 2 |
| 1.1.3 Import files | Part 2 |
| 1.1.4 Open non-native files directly in Word | Part 1, Topic 1-A |
| 1.1.5 Open a PDF in Word for editing | Part 1, Topic 1-A |
| **1.2 Navigate through a Document** | |
| 1.2.1 Search for text within document | Part 1, Topic 2-C |
| 1.2.2 Insert hyperlinks | Part 3 |
| 1.2.3 Create bookmarks | Part 3 |
| 1.2.4 Demonstrate how to use Go To | Part 1, Topic 2-C |
| **1.3 Format a Document** | |
| 1.3.1 Modify page setup | Part 1, Topic 7-D |
| 1.3.2 Change document themes | Part 2 |
| 1.3.3 Change document style sets | Part 1, Topic 3-F |
| 1.3.4 Insert simple headers and footers | Part 1, Topic 7-C |
| 1.3.5 Insert watermarks | Part 1, Topic 7-B |
| 1.3.6 Insert page numbers | Part 1, Topic 7-C |
| **1.4 Customize Options and Views for Documents** | |
| 1.4.1 Change document views | Part 1, Topic 1-A |
| 1.4.2 Demonstrate how to use zoom | Part 1, Topic 1-A |
| 1.4.3 Customize the Quick Access toolbar | Part 1, Topic 9-A |

| Objective Domain | Covered In |
|---|---|
| 1.4.4 Customize the Ribbon | Part 1, Topic 9-A |
| 1.4.5 Split the window | Part 1, Topic 1-A |
| 1.4.6 Add values to document properties | Part 3 |
| 1.4.7 Demonstrate how to use Show/Hide | Part 1, Topic 1-B |
| 1.4.8 Record simple macros | Part 2 |
| 1.4.9 Assign shortcut keys | Part 2 |
| 1.4.10 Manage macro security | Part 2 |
| **1.5 Configure Documents to Print or Save** | |
| 1.5.1 Configure documents to print | Part 1, Topic 1-B |
| 1.5.2 Save documents in alternative file formats | Part 1, Topic 9-B |
| 1.5.3 Print document sections | Part 1, Topic 1- B |
| 1.5.4 Save files to remote locations | Part 1, Topic 1-B |
| 1.5.5 Protect documents with passwords | Part 3 |
| 1.5.6 Set print scaling | Part 1, Topic 1-B |
| 1.5.7 Maintain backward compatibility | Part 1, Topic 9-B |
| **2.0 Format Text, Paragraphs, and Sections** | |
| **2.1 Insert Text and Paragraphs** | |
| 2.1.1 Append text to documents | Part 1, Topic 1-B |
| 2.1.2 Find and replace text | Part 1, Topic 2-C |
| 2.1.3 Copy and paste text | Part 1, Topic 2-B |
| 2.1.4 Insert text via AutoCorrect | Part 1, Topic 9-A |
| 2.1.5 Remove blank paragraphs | Part 1, Topic 1-B |
| 2.1.6 Insert built-in fields | Part 1, Topic 7-C |
| 2.1.7 Insert special characters (©,™,£) | Part 1, Topic 6-A |
| **2.2 Format Text and Paragraphs** | |
| 2.2.1 Change font attributes | Part 1, Topic 3-A |
| 2.2.2 Demonstrate how to use Find and Replace to format text | Part 1, Topic 3-G |
| 2.2.3 Demonstrate how to use Format Painter | Part 1, Topic 3-A |
| 2.2.4 Set paragraph spacing | Part 1, Topic 3-D |
| 2.2.5 Set line spacing | Part 1, Topic 3-D |
| 2.2.6 Clear existing formatting | Part 1, Topic 3-G |
| 2.2.7 Set indentation | Part 1, Topic 3-B |
| 2.2.8 Highlight text selections | Part 1, Topic 3-A |
| 2.2.9 Add styles to text | Part 1, Topic 3-F |
| 2.2.10 Change text to WordArt | Part 2 |
| 2.2.11 Modify existing style attributes | Part 2 |

| Objective Domain | Covered In |
|---|---|
| **2.3 Order and Group Text and Paragraphs** | |
| 2.3.1 Prevent paragraph orphans | Part 2 |
| 2.3.2 Insert breaks to create sections | Part 2 |
| 2.3.3 Create multiple columns within sections | Part 2 |
| 2.3.4 Add titles to sections | Part 2 |
| 2.3.5 Force page breaks | Part 1, Topic 7-D |
| **3.0 Create Tables and Lists** | |
| **3.1 Create a Table** | |
| 3.1.1 Convert text to tables | Part 1, Topic 4-D |
| 3.1.2 Convert tables to text | Part 1, Topic 4-D |
| 3.1.3 Define table dimensions | Part 1, Topic 4-B |
| 3.1.4 Set AutoFit options | Part 1, Topic 4-D |
| 3.1.5 Demonstrate how to use Quick Tables | Part 1, Topic 4-A |
| 3.1.6 Set a table title | Part 1, Topic 4-B |
| **3.2 Modify a Table** | Part 2 |
| 3.2.1 Apply styles to tables | Part 1, Topic 4-C |
| 3.2.2 Modify fonts within tables | |
| 3.2.3 Sort table data | Part 2 |
| 3.2.4 Configure cell margins | Part 1, Topic 4-B |
| 3.2.5 Demonstrate how to apply formulas to a table | Part 2 |
| 3.2.6 Modify table dimensions | Part 1, Topic 4-B |
| 3.2.7 Merge cells | Part 1, Topic 4-B |
| **3.3 Create and Modify a List** | |
| 3.3.1 Add numbering or bullets | Part 1, Topic 3-C |
| 3.3.2 Create custom bullets | Part 1, Topic 5-C |
| 3.3.3 Modify list indentation | Part 1, Topic 5-C |
| 3.3.4 Modify line spacing | Part 1, Topic 3-D |
| 3.3.5 Increase and decrease list levels | Part 1, Topic 5-C |
| 3.3.6 Modify numbering | Part 1, Topic 5-B |
| **4.0 Apply References** | |
| **4.1 Create Endnotes, Footnotes, and Citations** | |
| 4.1.1 Insert endnotes | Part 3 |
| 4.1.2 Manage footnote locations | Part 3 |
| 4.1.3 Configure endnote formats | Part 3 |
| 4.1.4 Modify footnote numbering | Part 3 |
| 4.1.5 Insert citation placeholders | Part 3 |

| Objective Domain | Covered In |
|---|---|
| 4.1.6 Insert citations | Part 3 |
| 4.1.7 Insert bibliography | Part 3 |
| 4.1.8 Change citation styles | Part 3 |
| **4.2 Create Captions** | |
| 4.2.1 Add captions | Part 3 |
| 4.2.2 Set caption positions | Part 3 |
| 4.2.3 Change caption formats | Part 3 |
| 4.2.4 Change caption labels | Part 3 |
| 4.2.5 Exclude labels from captions | Part 3 |
| **5.0 Insert and Format Objects** | |
| **5.1 Insert and Format Building Blocks** | |
| 5.1.1 Insert Quick Parts | Part 2 |
| 5.1.2 Insert textboxes | Part 2 |
| 5.1.3 Demonstrate how to use Building Blocks Organizer | Part 2 |
| 5.1.4 Customize Building Blocks | Part 2 |
| **5.2 Insert and Format Shapes and SmartArt** | |
| 5.2.1 Insert simple shapes | Part 2 |
| 5.2.2 Insert SmartArt | Part 1, Topic 6-B; Part 2 |
| 5.2.3 Modify SmartArt properties (color, size, shape) | Part 2 |
| 5.2.4 Wrap text around shapes | Part 2 |
| 5.2.5 Position shapes | Part 2 |
| **5.3 Insert and Format Images** | |
| 5.3.1 Insert images | Part 1, Topic 6-B |
| 5.3.2 Apply artistic effects | Part 2 |
| 5.3.3 Apply picture effects | Part 2 |
| 5.3.4 Modify image properties (color, size, shape) | Part 2 |
| 5.3.5 Add Quick Styles to images | Part 1, Topic 6-B |
| 5.3.6 Wrap text around images | Part 2 |
| 5.3.7 Position images | Part 2 |

# B | Microsoft Office Word 2013 Expert Exam 77-419

Selected Logical Operations courseware addresses Microsoft Office Specialist (MOS) certification skills for Microsoft Office 2013. The following table indicates where Word 2013 skills that are tested on Exam 77-419 are covered in the Logical Operations Microsoft Office Word 2013 series of courses.

| Objective Domain | Covered In |
| --- | --- |
| **1.0 Manage and Share Documents** | |
| **1.1 Manage Multiple Documents** | |
| 1.1.1 Modify existing templates | Part 2 |
| 1.1.2 Merge multiple documents | Part 3 |
| 1.1.3 Manage versions of documents | Part 1, Topic 9-B |
| 1.1.4 Copy styles from template to template | Part 2 |
| 1.1.5 Open a PDF in Word for editing | Part 1, Topic 1-A |
| 1.1.6 Copy macros from document to document | Part 2 |
| 1.1.7 Link to external data | Part 3 |
| 1.1.8 Move building blocks between documents | Part 2 |
| **1.2 Prepare Documents for Review** | |
| 1.2.1 Set tracking options | Part 3 |
| 1.2.2 Limit authors | Part 3 |
| 1.2.3 Restrict editing | Part 3 |
| 1.2.4 Delete document draft version | Part 1, Topic 9-B |
| 1.2.5 Remove document metadata | Part 3 |
| 1.2.6 Mark as final | Part 3 |
| 1.2.7 Protect a document with a password | Part 3 |
| **1.3 Manage Document Changes** | |
| 1.3.1 Track changes | Part 3 |
| 1.3.2 Manage comments | Part 3 |

| Objective Domain | Covered In |
|---|---|
| 1.3.3 Demonstrate how to use markup options | Part 3 |
| 1.3.4 Resolve multi-document style conflicts | Part 3 |
| 1.3.5 Display all changes | Part 3 |
| **1.0 Design Advanced Documents** | |
| **2.1 Apply Advanced Formatting** | |
| 2.1.1 Demonstrate how to use wildcards in find and replace searches | Part 1, Topic 2-C |
| 2.1.2 Create custom field formats | Part 2 |
| 2.1.3 Set advanced layout options | Part 2 |
| 2.1.4 Set character space options | Part 2 |
| 2.1.5 Set advanced character attributes | Part 2 |
| 2.1.6 Create and break section links | Part 2 |
| 2.1.7 Link textboxes | Part 2 |
| **2.2 Apply Advanced Styles** | |
| 2.2.1 Create custom styles | Part 2 |
| 2.2.2 Customize settings for existing styles | Part 2 |
| 2.2.3 Create character-specific styles | Part 2 |
| 2.2.4 Assign keyboard shortcuts to styles | Part 2 |
| **2.3 Apply Advanced Ordering and Grouping** | |
| 2.3.1 Create outlines | Part 3 |
| 2.3.2 Promote sections in outlines | Part 3 |
| 2.3.3 Create master documents | Part 3 |
| 2.3.4 Insert subdocuments | Part 3 |
| 2.3.5 Link document elements | Part 3 |
| **3.0 Create Advanced References** | |
| **3.1 Create and Manage Indexes** | |
| 3.1.1 Create indexes | Part 3 |
| 3.1.2 Update indexes | Part 3 |
| 3.1.3 Mark index entries | Part 3 |
| 3.1.4 Demonstrate how to use index auto-mark files | Part 3 |
| **3.2 Create and Manage Reference Tables** | |
| 3.2.1 Create a table of contents | Part 3 |
| 3.2.2 Create a table of figures | Part 3 |
| 3.2.3 Format table of contents | Part 3 |
| 3.2.4 Update a table of authorities | Part 3 |
| 3.2.5 Set advanced reference options (captions, footnotes, citations) | Part 3 |

| Objective Domain | Covered In |
|---|---|
| **3.3 Manage Forms, Fields, and Mail Merge Operations** | |
| 3.3.1 Add custom fields | Part 2 |
| 3.3.2 Modify field properties | Part 2 |
| 3.3.3 Add field controls | Part 2 |
| 3.3.4 Modify field control properties | Part 2 |
| 3.3.5 Perform mail merges | Part 2 |
| 3.3.6 Manage recipient lists | Part 2 |
| 3.3.7 Insert merged fields | Part 2 |
| 3.3.8 Preview results | Part 2 |
| **4.0 Create Custom Word Elements** | |
| **4.1 Create and Modify Building Blocks** | |
| 4.1.1 Create custom building blocks | Part 2 |
| 4.1.2 Save selections as Quick Parts | Part 2 |
| 4.1.3 Edit building block properties | Part 2 |
| 4.1.4 Delete building blocks | Part 2 |
| **4.2 Create Custom Style Sets and Templates** | |
| 4.2.1 Create custom color themes | Part 2 |
| 4.2.2 Create custom font themes | Part 2 |
| 4.2.3 Create custom templates | Part 2 |
| 4.2.4 Create and manage style sets | Part 2 |
| **4.3 Prepare a document for Internationalization and Accessibility** | |
| 4.3.1 Configure language options in documents | Part 1, Topic 8-B |
| 4.3.2 Add alt-text to document elements | Part 1, Topic 8-C |
| 4.3.3 Create documents for use with accessibility tools | Part 1, Topic 8-C |
| 4.3.4 Manage multiple options for +Body and +Heading fonts | Part 2 |
| 4.3.5 Demonstrate how to apply global content standards | Part 1, Topic 8-C |
| 4.3.6 Modify Tab order in document elements and objects | Part 1, Topic 8-C |

# C | Microsoft Word 2013 Common Keyboard Shortcuts

The following table lists common keyboard shortcuts you can use in Word 2013.

| Function | Shortcut |
|---|---|
| Open a document | Ctrl + O |
| Create a new document | Ctrl + N |
| Save a document | Ctrl + S |
| Undo an action | Ctrl + Z |
| Redo or repeat an action | Ctrl + Y |
| Bold the selected text | Ctrl + B |
| Italicize the selected text | Ctrl + I |
| Underline the selected text | Ctrl + U |
| Copy the selected text | Ctrl + C |
| Paste the copied text | Ctrl + V |
| Open the **Navigation** pane to search a document | Ctrl + F |
| Switch to print preview | Alt + Ctrl + I |
| Print a document | Ctrl + P |
| Insert a review comment | Alt + Ctrl + M |
| Go to the beginning of a document | Home |
| Go to the end of a document | End |
| Insert a hyperlink | Ctrl + K |
| Insert a line break | Shift + Enter |
| Insert a page break | Ctrl + Enter |
| Insert a column break | Ctrl + Shift + Enter |
| Change the case of the selected letters | Shift + F3 |
| Capitalize all selected letters | Ctrl + Shift + A |
| Preview a mail merge | Alt + Shift + K |

| Function | Shortcut |
| --- | --- |
| Merge a document | Alt + Shift + N |

# Lesson Labs

Lesson labs are provided for certain lessons as additional learning resources for this course. Lesson labs are developed for selected lessons within a course in cases when they seem most instructionally useful as well as technically feasible. In general, labs are supplemental, optional unguided practice and may or may not be performed as part of the classroom activities. Your instructor will consider setup requirements, classroom timing, and instructional needs to determine which labs are appropriate for you to perform, and at what point during the class. If you do not perform the labs in class, your instructor can tell you if you can perform them independently as self-study, and if there are any special setup requirements.

# Lesson Lab 3-1
## Formatting Text and Paragraphs

**Activity Time: 15 minutes**

### Data Files

C:\091024Data\Formatting Text and Paragraphs\Newsletter content.docx

### Scenario

You are working on a document that will later be used as a newsletter for Bit by Bit Fitness. Other coworkers have contributed content, and you want to start formatting the text and paragraphs so that the document begins to look more professional.

1. From the **C:\091024Data\Formatting Text and Paragraphs** folder, open **Newsletter content.docx**, and save it in the current folder as *My Newsletter content.docx*

2. Change the font for the entire document to **Arial, 12 pt**.

3. On the first page, apply the **Heading 1** style to "Newsletter content ideas."

4. Apply the **Heading 2** style to "Fit tip of the month," "Events," "Recipe of the Month," "Winners of Our April Fitness Challenge!," "BitWits Monthly Meeting," "Testimonials," and "Fitness Class Schedule."

5. In the "Recipe of the Month" section, italicize "Ingredients" and "Directions."

6. Create a bulleted list from the "Ingredients" items.

7. Create a numbered list for the recipe directions.

8. Add a new list item to "Directions" with the text *Serve immediately with lemon wedges.*

9. Apply a plain box border and light orange shading to the two paragraphs under "Testimonials."

10. Save and close the document.

# Lesson Lab 4-1
## Adding Tables

**Activity Time:** 15 minutes

### Data Files

C:\091024Data\Adding Tables\Newsletter content.docx

### Scenario

The Fitness Class Schedule in the Newsletter content document needs some fine-tuning, and you want to make it "pop" for the reader, so you decide to apply a table style.

---

1. From the **C:\091024Data\Adding Tables** folder, open **Newsletter content.docx**, and save it in the current folder as *My Newsletter content.docx*

2. On the fourth page, in the Fitness Class Schedule table, move the **Saturday** column to the right of the **Friday** column.

3. If necessary, resize the columns so that the day names and class names fit correctly.

4. Apply the orange **Grid Table 2 - Accent 6** table style.

5. Add left and right borders to the table.

6. Add inside borders to the cells between the row and column headings.

7. Save and close the document.

---

# Lesson Lab 5-1
## Managing Lists

**Activity Time: 15 minutes**

### Data Files

C:\091024Data\Managing Lists\Newsletter content.docx

### Scenario

You've noticed that the person who added the list of fitness challenge winners seems to have listed them out of order. You've also seen that the BitWits monthly meeting agenda needs to be formatted as a multilevel list so that it will make sense when given to the club members.

1. From the **C:\091024Data\Managing Lists** folder, open **Newsletter content.docx**, and save it in the current folder as *My Newsletter content.docx*

2. Under "Winners of Our April Fitness Challenge!," sort the list in ascending order, by place.

3. On the third page, create a multilevel list of the agenda items to match the following example.

1)→Purpose¶
    a)→Regular·scheduled·meeting¶

¶

2)→Old·Business¶
    a)→Approve·minutes·of·last·meeting¶
    b)→Budget·status·update¶

¶

3)→New·Business¶
    a)→Book·sale·July·30¶
       i)→ Volunteer·sign·up¶
       ii)→Where/when·to·receive·book·donations¶
    b)→Choose·next·month's·book¶

¶

4)→Book·Discussion¶
5)→Wrap·Up¶
    a)→Set·next·meeting·date¶

4. Save and close the document.

# Lesson Lab 6–1
## Inserting Graphic Objects

### Activity Time: 15 minutes

### Data Files

C:\091024Data\Inserting Graphic Objects\Newsletter content.docx

C:\091024Data\Inserting Graphic Objects\fish.png

### Scenario

You think the Recipe of the Month section could use a little brightening, so you decide to add a picture, then add that picture to a new clip art collection.

---

1. From the **C:\091024Data\Inserting Graphic Objects** folder, open **Newsletter content.docx**, and save it in the current folder as *My Newsletter content.docx*

2. Place the insertion point at the beginning of the line containing the text **Recipe of the Month**, and from the **C:\091024Data\Inserting Graphic Objects** folder, insert **fish.png**.

3. Set the position of the picture to **Middle Right with Square Text Wrapping**.

4. Place the insertion point on a blank line above the text "Recipe of the Month," and then search Office.com for a clip art image of a recipe and insert the desired image in the document.

5. Save and close the document.

---

# Lesson Lab 7-1
## Controlling Page Appearance

**Activity Time: 15 minutes**

### Data Files
C:\091024Data\Controlling Page Appearance\Newsletter content.docx

### Scenario
You'd like to add more design elements to the Newsletter content document to give it some polish. You decide to add a page border, then reset the margins, insert manual page breaks to keep heading information grouped together, and change the vertical alignment of the text.

1. From the **C:\091024Data\Controlling Page Appearance** folder, open **Newsletter content.docx**, and save it in the current folder as *My Newsletter content.docx*

2. Apply a box style, dotted line page border, in a light orange color.

3. Set the page margins to **Moderate**.

4. Insert manual page breaks before "Recipe of the Month" and "Winners of Our April Fitness Challenge!"

5. Set the vertical alignment of the text to **Center**.

6. Save and close the document.

# Lesson Lab 8–1

## Proofing a Document

**Activity Time: 15 minutes**

### Data Files

C:\091024Data\Proofing a Document\Newsletter content.docx

### Scenario

You need to run a spelling and grammar check. You would also like to find a replacement for a word before sharing the Newsletter content document with your coworkers.

---

1. From the **C:\091024Data\Proofing a Document** folder, open **Newsletter content.docx**, and save it in the current folder as *My Newsletter content.docx*

2. Check the document for spelling and grammar errors. Correct errors as you see fit.

3. On the first page, in the **Events** section, replace **Persons** with the synonym of your choice.

4. Save and close the document.

---

# Lesson Lab 9–1
## Customizing the Word Environment

**Activity Time: 15 minutes**

### Data Files
C:\091024Data\Customizing the Word Environment\Newsletter content.docx

### Scenario
Although you've already customized Word to some extent, you think you could add some more shortcuts to help increase your efficiency. Additionally, one of your coworkers has asked for a copy of the Newsletter content document in a different format.

1. Add the **Save As** command, and the **HOME** tab **Font** group to the **Quick Access Toolbar**.

2. Create an **AutoCorrect** entry to replace "bw" with "BitWits."

3. From the **C:\091024Data\Customizing the Word Environment** folder, open **Newsletter content.docx**, and save it in the current folder as *My Newsletter content.docx*

4. Run the **Compatibility Checker** on the document.

5. Save the document as a PDF file.

6. Open the PDF file in the PDF reader.

7. Close the PDF reader, and close **My Newsletter content.docx**.

# Glossary

**Backstage View**
The "behind the scenes" view of commands you can use to do file-related tasks, such as saving, opening, or printing a document.

**clipboard**
A temporary storage area for content that has been cut or copied from a document.

**Draft view**
A document view that shows the document without certain elements, such as graphics, or headers and footers.

**FILE tab**
The ribbon element that displays the **Backstage View**, where you can access commands that perform file-related tasks, such as saving and printing.

**gallery**
A collection of elements that belong to the same category, such as styles or effects.

**task pane**
An interface element that provides quick access to feature-specific options and commands.

**contextual tab**
Additional tabs that appear on the ribbon when you work with objects such as tables, pictures, or shapes.

**dialog box launcher**
A small button with a downward-pointing arrow, located in the bottom-right corner of some groups on the ribbon.

**document view**
A particular layout in which to view your document.

**field**
A defined area to be used for a specific type of information.

**file format**
The way the information in a file is encoded.

**font**
A set of characters with a specific style and size.

**footer**
A defined area at the bottom margin of a page where you can add textual or graphical information that is common to all or to some of the pages in a document.

**Format Painter**
A handy Word tool that helps you copy the formatting in selected text and apply it to one or more additional selections.

**formatting marks**
Nonprinting characters that display within the text to designate formatting elements such as spaces, tabs, and paragraph and line breaks.

### header

A defined area at the top margin of a page where you can add textual or graphical information that is common to all or to some of the pages in a document.

### HOME tab

The ribbon element that contains the frequently used commands you'll use to start working with a Word document.

### hyphenation

The use of the hyphen, a punctuation mark that joins separate words, or splits words by their syllables.

### indent

The amount of space between a margin and a line or paragraph.

### INSERT tab

The ribbon element that contains commands that insert different objects into your document, such as charts, tables, and pictures.

### landing page

The page to which Word 2013 opens. It contains a navigation pane and a list of templates you can use to create a new document. If it is the first time Word 2013 was run on your computer, you would see account and product information instead of the navigation pane and templates.

### line break

A way to end a line before it wraps to the following line, but without starting a new paragraph.

### Live Preview

A feature used to show certain formatting changes to your document before you actually apply them.

### MAILINGS tab

The ribbon element that contains commands to create mailing documents, such as faxes, letters, and emails.

### margin

The empty area along the top, bottom, left, and right edges of a page.

### Mini toolbar

The floating toolbar that appears when you select text in a document.

### multilevel list

A list with a hierarchical structure, wherein the number or bullet format is configured separately for each level of the list. Also known as a sublist.

### Outline view

A document view that shows the document data in a hierarchical mode, allowing you to insert and arrange topics and subtopics.

### PAGE LAYOUT tab

The ribbon element that contains commands used to customize document pages, including controlling the placement of text and graphics.

### paragraph alignment

The horizontal position of a paragraph relative to the left and right margins in a document.

### Print Layout view

A document view that shows the document as it will appear when printed.

### Quick Style set

A package of styles that work well together when applied as a group to text.

### Quick Tables

Preformatted tables that contain sample data.

### Read Mode

Shows a document in read-only, full-screen mode in which the document is scrolled side to side rather than up and down.

### REFERENCES tab

The ribbon element that contains commands to create references to the document content, such as footnotes and indexes.

### REVIEW tab

The ribbon element that contains commands to review and edit the content in a document.

## ScreenTip

Text that appears when you hover the mouse pointer over commands on the ribbon and certain other elements of the application window.

## selection bar

A region on the left margin of a document that is used to select text.

## SkyDrive

A Microsoft cloud service that enables you to access the files stored there from any device such as your office computer, home computer, smartphone, or tablet.

## sort field

A list item that can be used as the criteria for sorting a list.

## sort field separator

A character used to separate sort fields.

## special characters

Punctuation, spacing, or typographical characters that typically are not available on a standard keyboard. Ellipses ( ... ) or em dashes ( — ) are examples of special characters.

## symbols

Characters that can be used to represent an idea or a word, such as copyright, trademark, or registered trademark.

## table

A container that is used to organize text, numerical data, or graphics.

## thesaurus

A reference tool containing a collection of synonyms and antonyms.

## VIEW tab

The ribbon element that contains various commands to switch between different document views.

## Web Layout view

A document view that shows the document as it would appear in a web browser.

## window views

Document display options that allow you to perform such tasks as moving between open documents, viewing documents side by side, or arranging multiple documents in a single window.

## Word document

An electronic document created by the Word application.

## Word Help

A repository of information about the various tools and features of Word.

## Word style

A collection of appearance settings that can be applied to text with a single click.

# Index